INTEGRITY
COUNTS

INTEGRITY COUNTS

BRAD RAFFENSPERGER

Forefront
BOOKS

Integrity Counts

Copyright © 2021 Brad Raffensperger
Written in collaboration with Richard Parker

Published by Forefront Books.

Cover Design by Bruce Gore, Gore Studio Inc.
Interior Design by Juicebox Designs

ISBN: 978-1-63763-033-4 print
ISBN: 978-1-63763-034-1 e-book

To our eldest son Brenton, who passed more than three years ago.
Brenton loved politics, poetry, the great classical writers, and music,
and most importantly, he loved me and I loved him.
Brenton encouraged my first steps into the political arena and
brought perspectives that shed light on my blind spots.
We miss him and always will. I love you, Son.

With deep love,

Dad and Mom
June 2021

"This book will lose me some friends. But if it lost me all and gained me none, in God's name, as I am a free man, I would publish it."

—Sam Houston

CONTENTS

Introduction 11

Chapter 1: **Wait. Listen. Respect.** 14

Chapter 2: **Parents of a Prodigal Son**. 19

Chapter 3: **"Make Things a Little Bit Better"** 32

Chapter 4: **Unquestioned Integrity** 43

Chapter 5: **Cynical, Poll-Tested Strategies**. 57

Chapter 6: **Building a More Secure Voting System** 71

Chapter 7: **2020** 75

Chapter 8: **Sixty Days of Disinformation** 95

Chapter 9: **The Call** 164

Chapter 10: **The Aftermath: Our Hope** 205

Acknowledgments 227

Notes. 229

INTRODUCTION

I don't expect history to long remember the name Brad Raffensperger. I do, however, believe future generations of Americans will remember these times when a president who lost an election refused to concede and instead went about challenging the integrity of America's core democratic institutions. Calling into question state election procedures, he persuaded many of his supporters—with anger and indignation, but without real evidence—that he was the rightful winner. The political system and the courts alike rejected his claims, but many voters, fanned by the president's rhetoric, were convinced that those institutions were part of the problem, that the new chief executive was illegitimate, and the election system had failed them.

As secretary of state for the state of Georgia, I stood at times as subject, object, and target in the unfolding drama. In these pages, I will share my experience and observations with the hope my words might help rebuild confidence in our elections.

One of the most troubling questions in the wake of the 2020 election is whether we will see every candidate who loses a major election refuse to accept the results, and instead set out to raise money and build support on unfounded claims of fraud and corruption. To avoid that prospect, we must come to terms with the scope of the problem, but doing so won't be comfortable for either party.

I say "either party" because the 2020 crisis was not unprecedented in Georgia. By November 2020, I had been challenging the claims of a "stolen election" for nearly two years. From my perspective, the most striking aspect of the Trump ordeal was not its novelty, but the unshakable sense of déjà vu that dogged me throughout.

When President Donald Trump stood before a crowd near the White House on January 6, 2021, and proclaimed, "We will never concede. . . . You don't concede when there's theft involved,"[1] my mind leaped back to the fall of 2018, when Stacey Abrams, who had just lost the race for governor of Georgia, told a crowd of supporters, "So, to be clear, this is not a speech of concession. Concession means to acknowledge an action is right, true or proper. As a woman of conscience and faith, I cannot concede."[2] The similarities don't end there, and when considered with some care, they paint a troubling picture of an all-too-bipartisan willingness to undermine the integrity of our democracy, and the public's confidence in it, for the sake of personal, partisan, and financial gain.

A president of the United States has a unique responsibility to defend the Constitution, and President Trump's rallying of his supporters against the election results led to a violent attack against Congress and his own vice president at the Capitol. Abrams was not a sitting government official when she refused to concede her election, but as a major national figure, she had a distinct obligation to avoid slandering our electoral system. While her false charges (thankfully) did not lead to violence, they continue to be widely believed and repeated even now, particularly by people who claim to be concerned about the integrity of our democracy. The corrosive effects of such lies are spreading still.

These threats to public confidence from both sides of the political divide are at odds with the realities of American elections. The fact is this: Our elections are both fairer and more secure than they have been at any point in our history. Voter participation rates are high, and evidence of widespread fraud is exceedingly rare. And yet, thanks to irresponsible rhetoric from members of both parties, Americans are increasingly skeptical of their country's ability to hold free and fair elections.

To point to the breadth of the problem, therefore, is not to draw equivalences or to minimize or exaggerate the misbehavior of one person or party. It is, rather, to clarify the scope of the challenge confronting all those who want to restore faith in our democracy.

In 1981, Ronald Reagan began his first inaugural address by noting the significance of the peaceful transfer of power in our country:

> *The orderly transfer of authority as called for in the Constitution routinely takes place as it has for almost two centuries, and few of us stop to think how unique we really are. In the eyes of many in the world, this every-four-year ceremony we accept as normal is nothing less than a miracle.*[3]

That ceremony is the capstone of a complex, multilayered, decentralized process of running elections that are safe, accessible, reliable, and fair. Accomplishing it has never been a simple matter, but our country is actually quite good at it. The secrets to its success are fairness, trust, and integrity. Those three values are closely intertwined.

But we can no longer take that combination for granted, and we cannot treat the shortage of public confidence in our elections as the fault of one side or another alone. It is a problem that runs to the core of our civic culture. To address it, we all must acknowledge our role in causing it, and take on the hard work of building mutual trust by becoming more worthy of it.

CHAPTER 1
WAIT. LISTEN. RESPECT.

"HELLO, BRAD AND RYAN AND EVERYBODY. We appreciate the time and the call."

The voice on my cell phone speaker belonged to President Donald Trump. My wife, Tricia, and I sat at our kitchen counter with the phone in a metal stand so I could take notes as we listened.

My first thought when I heard the president's voice was, *What would my dad think of this? His son is talking to the president of the United States.*

But this was no time for wandering thoughts. I knew why the president was calling, and I needed to focus. He got right to the point. "So, we've spent a lot of time on this," he said, "and if we could just go over some of the numbers, I think it's pretty clear that we won. We won very substantially in Georgia."

I was tempted to interrupt, to offer a correction, but then I heard my dad's voice in my head.

Wait. Listen. Respect.

So I listened and waited for an invitation to respond.

It was Saturday afternoon, January 2, 2021, sixty days after the presidential election. Beginning long before the election and every day since, President Trump had attacked the foundation of our democracy and undermined Americans' faith in our electoral institutions. He had tweeted insults and threats at me and at Georgia Governor Brian Kemp. Now he was directly attacking the election itself. He was asking me, as Georgia's secretary of state, to "find 11,780 votes"—enough for him to claim a win in our state.

I could not do that, because the data didn't support it. In my analysis, this was a physical impossibility; there were not 11,780 votes to be found. Since assuming office in January 2019, my team and I focused our efforts to head off every possible avenue for election fraud. Proactively, in early 2020 right after COVID-19 hit, I created the Absentee Ballot Fraud Task Force because I fully expected more voters would want to vote from the safety of their homes rather than risk going out and voting in a public setting. I was chastised in the press by prominent Democrats for that decision. The task force members consisting of conservative Republicans, Democrats, and independents had strong election integrity and legal backgrounds to help ensure robust security measures were in place in Georgia.

I voted for President Trump, and I am a lifelong conservative Republican with a proven voting record to match. But I could not do what he asked, because the numbers just weren't there. My job as secretary of state is to oversee fair and honest elections for everyone. Was I disappointed in the outcome? Yes. Could I change the outcome? No.

Our nation and our democracy have survived for nearly two and a half centuries because we hold free and fair elections secured with integrity. It's the ultimate "trust-but-verify" system, with multiple layers of technology and oversight to prevent fraud. We count and accurately record every legal vote. We recount when necessary, and we cannot be persuaded to report anything but the facts. Not by the president. Not by anybody.

Questions and cynicism about our elections in recent years have diminished trust from both Republicans and Democrats. Some falsely believed that Russian hackers altered votes in the 2016 presidential election and allowed Trump to defeat Hillary Clinton. Some Georgia Democrats made false claims that voters were suppressed or that problems with voting machines allowed Republican Brian Kemp to defeat Democrat Stacey Abrams in the 2018 gubernatorial election in Georgia.

Although the idea was not original to him, Trump's attack on our electoral system was louder and more destructive by orders of magnitude than any that preceded it.

Earlier in the day, Neil Cavuto had interviewed me for *Cavuto Live* on Fox News. I had driven to a studio in northeast Atlanta where he spoke with me on the air from New York. "You are secretary of state," he said. "You're also Republican. So you have an interest in the Republicans running."[4]

A moment later he said again, "You are a Republican, and you've announced your support for the Republican candidates in the past."[5] Then he asked me about the presidential election results and wondered how Joe Biden could have received 12 million more votes nationally than Barack Obama.

My response was similar to what I had been saying since November.

I told Cavuto that I couldn't address the results in the other states, only in Georgia, and I explained why the votes did not add up to a win for President Trump. "Here are the facts," I said. "Twenty thousand Republican voters, traditional Republican voters [who had voted in the June primary] just skipped the presidential race. Senator David Perdue got 19,000 more votes in the metro regions [of Atlanta and Athens] than President Trump did. And in our Republican congressional areas, [Georgia's Republican candidates] got 33,000 more votes than President Trump."[6]

Thousands of Georgians had voted for Republican candidates down the ballot, but for Biden at the top of the ticket.

If President Trump had been as popular as Senator Perdue in the suburbs, he would have carried Georgia. If 20,000 Republicans who voted in June had shown up in November, Trump would have carried Georgia. If President Trump had polled as well as Republican congressional candidates in Republican districts, he would have easily won Georgia. And truth be told, my life, my family's lives, and my staff's lives would have been a lot calmer and safer. He still wouldn't have won the presidency, but Georgia would not have been his whipping post. It's sad to have to admit that the state GOP badly lost the organizational and ground game to the Democratic Party.

To confirm the accuracy of the results, we recounted every legal ballot in every county by machine and by hand—just over 5 million of them. We brought in Georgia Bureau of Investigation experts to augment our secretary of state investigator staff auditing signatures on absentee ballot envelopes. Every count, recount, and audit led to the same result: Biden received more votes than Trump in Georgia.

I drove home after the interview, and around lunchtime the deputy secretary of state, Jordan Fuchs, called and said, "President Trump saw you on Fox News this morning. Mark Meadows called me and said he wants to talk to you." Meadows was the president's chief of staff.

"The president wants to talk to me?"

"Yes, sir."

Since the election, Trump had called into question Georgia's election procedures almost daily, and he persuaded many of his supporters—with anger and indignation, but without evidence— that he was the rightful winner. He took his claims to court and was rejected on the facts. On the last day of 2020, Trump had filed *Trump v. Kemp and Raffensperger*, a lawsuit against Governor Kemp and me directing us to decertify the valid results of the presidential election in Georgia.

I told Jordan that I was reluctant to take the president's call with the lawsuit hanging over us. She said Meadows was insistent, so I agreed, but I said, "I don't think it's appropriate for just the president and me to be on the line. I want you and Ryan to be on the call too." Ryan Germany was the general counsel in our office. They both needed to hear everything that would be said.

As I agreed to take the call, I anticipated the tone of it. I had an idea of what to expect from President Trump. He's a real estate developer, and I've dealt with dozens of developers in my career. I am a structural engineer, and my company provides high-strength steel for construction projects. I'm a subcontractor. When I'm on a job site, the developer is at the top of the food chain, and when the developer is having an issue, whatever it is, it all rolls downhill to the general contractor and then to the subcontractor. The conversation might start off friendly, then they turn up the pressure, and if they don't get what they want—which usually means "at no additional cost or extension of time to the schedule"—it can become a one-way, high-volume conversation. Trump was the developer, and I was the subcontractor.

Jordan called Meadows, and he agreed to our conditions. They scheduled the call for three o'clock. Perhaps, I thought hopefully, I could lay out the facts, and this would be the beginning of the end of the turmoil.

It wasn't.

CHAPTER 2

PARENTS OF A PRODIGAL SON

CONSTANTLY, TRICIA AND I ARE ASKED why we remained calm through all of this. "How can you just respond without anger or resentment?"

That's because to know us is to know our story.

Everyone has a story. When I know a person's story, I have a better idea about what makes them tick, what is important to them, and why. For the next two chapters, with Tricia's help, I'd like to share some of ours.

A big component of my story—and how and why I had the strength to stand resolutely against the onslaught of misinformation, disinformation, outright lies, and derogatory name-calling—is reflected in my parents, who raised and instilled timeless values in my siblings and me: grit, honesty, courage, integrity, hard work, respect, loyalty, faithfulness, manners, perseverance. Grit and perseverance get you through far worse things in life than this election and a president who felt that bullying the secretary of state of Georgia was his only means to change the outcome. (Even if I had acquiesced to his demands, Georgia was but one state, and he needed at least two more to change the final outcome.)

"I've been through worse" became our motto in the weeks and months following the 2020 election. Anyone who has lost a child knows there is nothing on earth more heart-wrenching, life-changing, and devastating. That's real life, that's real hurt, and nothing can come close to that kind of loss. Sadly, I also know that we are not alone out there. Many families, like us, have been ravaged by the epidemic of addiction. Many parents, spouses, siblings, and children have lost a loved one to this dreaded disease.

Our pain also comes from the many people who have recently turned their backs on us without the benefit of an explanation, just as others did in the early stages of our son's addiction. It was a road we were all too familiar with.

We have experienced how quickly and easily decisions and judgments can be made based on the lack of knowledge and facts. Addiction is a disease and is simply not in anyone's control. Our son was an addict, but that did not make him *less than*, and it did not make us bad parents. Now, as then, we stayed the course.

As the election outcome became a focus of national news, I knew we had the facts, and I knew over time the truth would be revealed and believed. Of course, Tricia did too. She had agreed to limited media interviews, where she explained that we are simply real people who love our family, have worked hard to build a business, and believe in the American way that putting your nose to the grindstone can get you to a better place in this life.

"Brad also believed he could make a difference in politics," Tricia says. "I love my husband enough to know that his passion and belief in that was enough for me to give him the green light to pursue that dream. So when people ask how we maintained our composure when

Trump was tweeting at Brad or telling the media and the world from the White House that he was 'an enemy of the people,' I knew that these were words of insincerity and were untrue. President Trump doesn't know us at all. He assumed we would blindly roll over to any requests he had because he labeled us and called us names."

You may have been through worse too. You may have lost someone you loved during 2020 when we lost so many. We all face life events more difficult than having somebody call us names, even if that someone is the president.

The *worse* for us was losing our oldest son three years ago. Brenton had fought drug and alcohol addiction from the time he was fifteen years old. His life was a roller coaster of clean and sober, then using; clean and sober, then using; incarceration, then clean and sober. At twenty-six he was diagnosed with stage 3B Hodgkin's lymphoma, cancer in lymph nodes and cancerous tumors above and below his diaphragm. There were days fighting cancer when he told us he just wanted to die, and there were times when the pain drove him back into his addiction. Day after day and month after month and year after year, we prayed for a healing miracle . . . until the day we got that proverbial knock on the door to find out he had died of an overdose of fentanyl.

Yes, we've been through worse.

We prayed every day for twenty-three years for our son to stay clean and sober, for God to heal him. He didn't answer our prayers the way we wanted, but He was always there to walk with us.

It's hard to understand why our prayers aren't answered when we lose something so precious, when we pray so fervently for so long. And yet, as I say, God was with us.

Despite the loss of our son, God has given Tricia and me a sense of peace I cannot explain, because I do not understand it. All I know is that we *experience* it every day. God has also given us strength beyond anything we could ask for or even imagine—strength to endure every parent's worst nightmare. Again, I do not understand, but I am grateful.

Even with that strength and peace, there were days when we could relate to the Old Testament prophet Habakkuk, who wrote:

> *How long, Lord, have I called for help,*
> *And You do not hear?*
> *I cry out to You, "Violence!"*
> *Yet You do not save.* (Habakkuk 1:2, NASB)

We prayed for that peace and strength again when President Trump turned his attention toward me. We were barraged with messages that came in every form. Phone calls. Texts. Emails. Letters. Unexpected visitors. Tweets. Protestors chanting and waving homemade signs. Strange vehicles driving slowly past our home. We knew full well that in the aftermath of the 2020 election, because of President Trump's rhetoric and encouraged by his vitriol, followers of his could attempt to harm us. Unbelievably, they threatened us and our children in the name of Jesus if we did not do their bidding.

In what world or state is it okay or sanctioned to threaten lives over political differences?

On a quiet Sunday morning in April 2021, two weeks after Easter, Tricia picked up her cell phone. A message had come in overnight from American@jesus.com:

> *please pray. we plan for the death of you and your family every day.*
> *Im sorry.*

It was another of many, many threatening texts. Certainly not the first, and probably not the last that we will receive. Family members of a secretary of state receive death threats . . . why? Because I choose to serve? Because I choose to tell the truth? Is this the United States?

As the many death threats and sexualized threats to Tricia came to her phone to try to get me to change the election results, we persisted with our faith. We leaned in to a God who is always there and alongside each of us.

We know most of the threats are empty. We've also seen with our own eyes the threats that are legitimate. In those times, God becomes even more real to us. God is with us. He shows up in the most unexpected places.

People ask how I maintained my composure in the face of the threats from President Trump. Because of God's presence, God's peace, and God's strength. And because of the enduring love of Tricia, my family, my friends, and kind supporters—many of whom were total strangers, not just from Georgia but around the country—who sent messages of encouragement. As many evil threats poured in, so, too, did messages from people all over the country as they lifted us in prayer.

Through it all, we stood firm in our faith and our trust in God. Tricia says:

> *If there is one thing I want to add to our personal narrative, it is that we are just regular people. People with an abiding faith in God, people who have been molded and formed by the people we have known and loved. Brad and I were married forty-five years ago this year. We met in high school, and we experienced life together. Fortunately, we grew together and not apart as life threw us the many challenges it does. Are there things we would redo if we could? Sure there are. Life is never perfect, and neither are we.*

> *We have worked hard over the years running our own businesses and striving for the American dream, failing, winning, picking ourselves back up and starting again, persisting, and persisting some more. And then somewhere in between trying to raise three*

sons the best we knew how. I can say today I have been blessed and am forever thankful that we met and journeyed this life together.

I believe the statement, "What you see is what you get." I don't play any games. I represent who I am and no one else. Our marriage is like anyone else's marriage after forty-five years, with the usual ups and downs, its trials, its happy times, and its sad times. But through it all, I have never once questioned the integrity or honesty of this man I married. He has been faithful in all ways and true to me unquestionably.

So it is with difficulty that I search to understand how, without any facts, figures, or evidence, a person of such high position can slander and question my husband's integrity. How do people who do not know us accuse us of such treachery? Who has come forth to ask the questions? Who has made any effort to get to the truth? Who believes what they are told without facts or figures? So yes, these times are trying for our family and ourselves.

But we have one another, and we have God's presence in the midst of it all. And God alone knows our hearts and minds and our dreams, and that's all that matters. So we stand, we stand together, and we stand not alone.

◆ ◆ ◆

During one interview, I mentioned to the reporter that "President Trump doesn't know my story." In another interview, I reflected about the basic values that my father instilled in me, like honesty.

My father was an honorable man, born and raised in the western Pennsylvania mountain town of Johnstown, where hunting, fishing, and all things outdoors—and, of course, Friday night varsity football—were king. Those interests were passed along to me. Although his father was an architect, there was virtually no new work during the 1930s, so his parents watched every penny, did without, and grew a garden like many Americans during those hard years. My dad enlisted in the Navy in 1944 as soon as he finished high school. After World War II, the GI bill enabled him to go to college and earn an engineering degree. He never felt as if he was a genius, but he had an awful lot of common sense, he was good in math and science, and he had an incredible work ethic. He and others of that generation were hard workers. Though he was successful, he always worked for a company and never controlled his own destiny. My mom was my dad's biggest cheerleader. She always said that although he was the number two guy in the company, the company couldn't run without my father. She also had her hands full with me, my three sisters, and my brother. Yet between all the demands, she found time to paint. I still have one of those paintings—two boys catching and throwing a baseball. Vintage Norman Rockwell-style. Awesome.

When I was in grade school, my parents went to auctions and collected antique furniture. Much of that had to be refinished, and I watched as my mom spent hours on it. I have several of those pieces, and when Tricia and I were a young and broke married couple, I refinished several pieces of furniture myself so we had a table to eat at and chairs to sit on.

When I finished the fourth grade in Sinking Spring, Pennsylvania, Dad was transferred to Ontario, Canada, so we loaded into the family car for our new adventure.

My dad always found time for hunting and fishing, and I was his young understudy. Over the years we had great fun, and when the fish weren't biting or the bucks weren't on the move, I learned patience, hours of it. Patience to wait.

Coming from coal and steel country and with humble roots, my dad always had a heart for the "little guy." Today it is called the forgotten man. Hardworking, taxpaying, God-loving, salt-of-the-earth people.

He believed that a "man should be paid an honest day's pay for an honest day's work," so he had no problem if his craft workers were paid a good hourly wage, as long as they worked hard and produced.

My dad believed that you played the game to win within the rules and may the best team win. When you won, you accepted the win gracefully; if you lost, you shook your opponent's hand and lost gracefully.

He was a quiet, humble man, and my mom was more outgoing. Her father was an electrician and a Republican. At the kitchen table, my parents shared their opinions about politics and politicians. My father always told us you couldn't believe everything you read in the newspapers and you had to learn to think for yourself. He was not argumentative—all of our neighbors and coworkers really liked my dad—but he drew lines in the sand. He didn't like bullies or bullying.

I was in middle school when my parents started building their new house. One day when we were visiting to check on the progress of construction, a group of high school boys on the road in front of our house was trying to steal something from another high school kid. Pretty soon that gang was pushing the other kid around. That's when my father walked over to them and told them to shove off, and they did.

Before we moved to a new town, my dad scouted for a new church home. When the moving van showed up at our new house and we were unpacked, we had a place to go on Sunday. My father's simple faith gave me a foundation for my own faith to flourish later when I was in my early thirties.

These might seem like simple values that my parents passed along, but they are timeless, and they brought stability and guardrails to my thinking and my actions.

Similar, but on a much deeper and broader level, is my relationship with Tricia. Tricia started attending my high school when we were in the eleventh grade, and we began dating our senior year. She, too, was blessed to have parents who stood strong on values and who were friendly and outgoing, a trait Tricia shares. She is also incredibly creative and determined. We married when I was halfway through engineering school, and those last two years of school were wonderful. My grades went up, and I had my best friend with me all the time. Young with a tight financial budget, we had enough because we had each other. For forty-five years now, Tricia and I have been meshed together as we lived out our story.

A few years after graduation, I worked for a construction company in Virginia, which transferred us to Atlanta in 1982. Like my father, I was working for another company, but I knew that when the right opportunity arose, I would own my own company.

In the meantime, we had two sons, Brenton and Kyle, and I had a great idea for setting Tricia up in business. "You have a background in early childhood education," I said. "What if instead of you working in a childcare center, we bought a center and then you would run it? Brenton and Kyle would be with you during the day, and it would be a real estate investment with a business."

We found an existing daycare center in Lilburn, and we bought it. The owner was licensed for about 140 children, but they only had sixty-five enrolled. Over the next two years, we renovated the facility, and Tricia expanded the license to 174 children and had it running at full capacity.

A few years later, when the company I worked for began promoting people who were in the northern Virginia headquarters, I realized my upward progression was done since we had no interest in leaving Georgia and moving back to Virginia. We had planted our roots deep into Georgia soil.

The daycare center provided enough of a financial margin in our life for me to start my own company, and I connected with a colleague in the industry whose background was installation. We opened for business on October 19, 1987, the day now known as Black Monday—the largest one-day percentage drop for the Dow Jones Industrial Average in history. It was an inauspicious day to start a company, but we remained optimistic.

We designed, supplied, and installed post-tensioned steel along with rebar installation, and for several years, I was selling all day and designing after dinner at night. On weekends, I would do all of the estimates for the next week's bidding schedule. We found a lot of condominium construction opportunities along the Florida Gulf Coast and in Orlando, up in the Carolinas, and in Nashville and Birmingham. Between all that, I made sure I found time as the boys grew to coach their youth league basketball teams. In 1990, our youngest son, Jay, was born, and our roots further deepened in Georgia. In 1992, my parents retired to Georgia to be closer to our family and two of my sisters.

◆ ◆ ◆

In 2000, my business partner's health was failing, and I bought his share of the company, tying up a lot of cash to do so. Just a few years later, an abrupt change in worldwide steel put my company at risk financially. Around 2003, the International Trade Commission agreed with the U.S. Department of Commerce that foreign steel strand suppliers were dumping product in the United States. They responded by blocking those foreign producers from the U.S. market with large duties. Steel prices increased 40 percent overnight. Because this was a specialized slice of the total steel market, few outside of our industry were aware of this escalation.

Prestressed steel strand was the heart of our business. We had bid all our contracts before the price escalation, and we couldn't pass the increase through to our customers, contractors, and developers. It was my problem, not theirs.

Everybody knew what was going on. People in the industry know when you are going through a tough time, and it's like hanging your dirty laundry out there on the clothesline. The contractor had his own set of challenges: this job was costing him $20,000 a day in overhead, and like us, he had a lump-sum, fixed-price contract. If his upstream client didn't pay him, he couldn't pay us, and we'd all be out of luck. The contractor had to keep everything moving on schedule, and there was no one to pay for this unanticipated cost increase.

Under normal circumstances, a contractor might go to the developer and explain the situation. But in our case, the developer said, "I've got a $100 million building here. I've set my pro forma with the bank. Price change is not my problem. You should have anticipated that."

Then the builder said to me, "I can't get you more money to pay for the increase. Sorry."

And it all flowed downstream. It was *my* problem.

We had 20 million feet of strand contracted to sell for jobs across the Southeast at twelve cents per foot, and overnight the price went up to sixteen cents. So that alone was $800,000 in lost profits—our profit for an entire year.

We were a small company with just-in-time product—almost no inventory to cushion a dramatic price increase. We were operating at the limit of our line of credit, so we could not borrow more money to secure strand from new suppliers that would not offer me credit terms. Our strand consumption for seventy-five days would require $1 million that I did not have and could not borrow. Without cash, I couldn't get the raw steel materials to manufacture and ship to jobsites, so I had to give up a lot of contracts.

It got worse.

Subcontractors like me invoice contractors as the project progresses, and contractors pay sixty to seventy-five days after receiving the invoice. Contracts are written so that if the subcontractor gives up the contract, it is immediately void, and the contractor keeps the money he owes as an offset to pay someone else to finish the job. In other words, if he owed me $150,000 for work and materials and I didn't complete the job, he could cancel the contract and pay me nothing.

We had several contractors who shrugged, turned their backs, and took that route. Maybe I could have sued them, but nobody wins in court.

Thankfully, we were also working with a few contractors in Birmingham, Naples, and Myrtle Beach who hung with us. They kept us on the job and actually prepaid for strand at the higher price. You remember things like that. I would do anything now, over fifteen years later, to help out those contractors if they ever call me.

Coming out of that tough spot with my tail feathers singed, I determined never to go through that pain again. We rebuilt the company slowly. We were active in our church and Sunday school class, and I got involved in the men's ministry. Within a year, I became the leader of the group. We brought in a three-year program that was about real life—being authentic, how to win both at work and at home, and setting a vision for the great adventure, which is the life we are called to live. I became a voracious reader of business management books, and a close friend invited me to join a business owners peer group.

That tough time of 2003 to 2004 set the table and prepared me to navigate through the Great Recession of 2009 onward. In the construction industry, the period from 2009 to 2011 was a depression, and several solid companies did not survive. I entered with legacy debt in 2008 and exited in 2012 with our company virtually debt free. The earlier hard lessons paid off for us.

During the COVID-19 pandemic in 2020, my son Kyle, who is now our company president, and his team applied those same principles. Kyle has modeled how to build successful work teams while maintaining work-life balance. We have faced those obstacles just like so many other businesses and are thankful to have navigated those choppy seas.

Those challenging times we survived deepened my heart for all small business owners. Perhaps because I have lived through several hard business cycles, I understand how those hard times and crazy economic cycles challenge many small business owners. All small business owners, be they manufacturing, construction, restaurants and hospitality, or farmers and ranchers, share much in common. We sign personal guarantees for our bank loans and sign everyone's paychecks. We are not deeply capitalized like publicly traded companies, so we don't have the financial resources to weather major economic disruptions such as the Great Recession and COVID-19 like the big boys can. Yet small business owners and entrepreneurs are America's great engine of job creation. We need to keep them in the game for America to continue to move forward.

CHAPTER 3
"MAKE THINGS A LITTLE BIT BETTER"

POLITICALLY SPEAKING, I'M A LATE BLOOMER. I was fifty-six years old in 2010 when I first ran for office—an open seat on the Johns Creek City Council. Johns Creek, in north Fulton County, had been incorporated just five years earlier. The city was not divided into geographic districts for the city council; every council member was elected at large. With 25,000 households in the city, that meant knocking on a lot of doors.

When I began campaigning, several people congratulated me, even though I hadn't yet won a single vote. I asked one woman why the congratulations.

Her response was profound. "Brad," she said, "when anyone does more than just go along and does something extra, even if it is just stopping alongside the road to pick up some trash, that is to be saluted."

Her comment reminded me of two things: a note my son Jay had sent me two years earlier after I had told him I was considering political office and something Martin Luther King Jr. had said.

Jay had written:

I don't know how serious you are about the whole political career thing, but I just had an idea and I thought I should just send it to you. Our country was founded by a group of people who had dreams of a better future for their children. Why is it that no one operates on that basis anymore? The fact is that the world is pretty messy right now. Instead of trying to make the world a better place for us, why don't we try to make it a better place for the people who haven't even had a chance to make mistakes yet? Our country was founded with a legacy of selfless sacrifice, but somewhere along the way that ideal was lost. Why don't we restore that ideal? Why don't we focus on cleaning the world up as much as we can for our children's sake? It only takes a few to stand up. Last time a few stood up, more followed them. And those people founded the greatest country on earth.

I am proud of Jay for having the wisdom to share this with me. He has a heart for people and is incredibly kind and thoughtful. Over the years some of that has rubbed off on me. Kindness is a good thing. It doesn't make you soft; it just keeps you from being mean. And kindness is in short supply right now in many pockets of America.

When I ran for secretary of state a few years later, I mentioned this concept of running to "make things a little bit better." One of my competitors sniveled and denigrated that thought, as if I did not have big dreams, and we needed a big dreamer in that office. It's not that I don't dream big; it's that I consider it success when I "make things a little bit better."

Similarly, Dr. King said, "If I cannot do great things, I can do small things in a great way."

◆ ◆ ◆

Our son Brenton's journey brought us to an awareness of a major issue in our state and nation: the need for prison reform.

All criminals are not treated the same. Brenton was arrested for cocaine possession, and we had the resources to hire a lawyer. Then in 2004, a judge shook up his courtroom with an unusual sentence when Brenton was found guilty of possession and DUI. He sent Brenton back to prison, which would do nothing to help him deal with his addiction. And in addition to six months in prison—reduced because Brenton had completed another rehab program—the judge directed him to buy a casket at a funeral home and put it in his own home for six and a half years "as a reminder of the deadly consequences of your choices. I want you to be reminded every day that if you don't change your ways, you are a dead man."

Other nonviolent defendants in other courtrooms without good lawyers or family support in the courtroom received lengthier prison sentences. Over a twenty-year period, our state prison population doubled, in large part because of tougher sentencing for drug possession and nonviolent property crimes.

Brenton clarified the situation for me. "Nothing's really going to change," he said, "until over 50 percent of all the people being locked up are from white, middle-class families. Then you'll hear people say, 'Hey, what's going on here? My son is going to jail? He's not a criminal. He needs treatment!' Until then you won't see significant criminal justice reform."

Congress began considering the issue, with the possibility of creating a bipartisan National Criminal Justice Commission, and I wrote letters to legislators, congressmen, and senators. But Tricia and I were just garden-variety American citizens who worked jobs and paid our taxes. Our letters never made an impact, and Congress did not create the commission. I hoped I might have a louder voice as an elected official.

In December 2011, I was elected to the Johns Creek City Council in a runoff. Earlier that year, Nathan Deal was sworn in as Georgia's governor. With a friend's urging, I volunteered on the Deal campaign handing out candidate brochures, going to campaign meetings, and putting up yard signs. Governor Deal hinted in his January 2011 inaugural speech that he also wanted to reform our criminal justice system:

> *For violent and repeat offenders, we will make you pay for your crimes. For other offenders who want to change their lives, we will provide the opportunity to do so with day reporting centers; drug, DUI, and mental health courts; and expanded probation and treatment options. As a state, we cannot afford to have so many of our citizens waste their lives because of addictions. It is draining our state treasury and depleting our workforce.*[7]

The governor was singing our song. I will always have a soft spot in my heart for Governor Deal. He was the nation's leader in drug accountability courts.

In November 2014, Governor Deal appointed the state representative from our district to lead the Department of Revenue, and I ran for the open House seat and won in a runoff in January, after the 2015 General Assembly was already in session. Right away, I sponsored two bills that would allow homeowners to increase their homestead exemptions and reduce their property tax burdens.

A Bible study group met on Wednesday mornings at the capitol with House and Senate members, both Republicans and Democrats. The fellowship introduced me to a lot of legislators quickly. That personal time together studying God's Word and sharing our faith also built trust. When people reveal their faith walk, you begin to break down the walls that divide you, even if you still disagree on your politics.

The relationships I built working in the Georgia General Assembly showed me how both sides working together could accomplish good policies for all the people. A simple example of this is that in Washington, the Republicans' desks are on one side of the aisle, and the Democrats' desks are on the other. In the Georgia House, however, seating was randomly assigned, and my desk was between two Democrats, Erica Thomas and Patty Bentley. Representative Thomas grew up in foster homes in Tennessee and spoke passionately for at-risk children. Representative Bentley owned a small business and had been a county commissioner in middle Georgia for eight years. Over time, due to seating proximity, we had more opportunities for conversations and reached below the surface to find common ground in our faith and our love for our state and country.

More than once, the speaker of the house called for a vote on a bill I had sponsored, and Erica would look over and say, "Raffensperger, you know I love you, but . . ." just as she hit that red no button. I would smile and hit my green yes button. I understood where she came from, and I knew who she represented. She was going to vote the way she believed was best for her district, as I was for mine.

But when she saw me, she saw my humanity first. If our Christian faith tells us anything, it is to "love your neighbor as yourself." I believe she did.

I was as conservative as any member of the House, and though our votes almost never aligned, I enjoyed representing my constituents while sitting between and fellowshipping with these two Democrats.

During my time in the statehouse, I proposed and passed homeowner tax relief for seniors and everyone in my county. That was the first time I remember coming into contact with Stacey Abrams, as she was trying to tell her caucus not to vote for the local tax cut bill I had proposed. I got most of the Democrats to support my bill, and it passed and went over to the Senate, where it was blocked by a now Stop the Steal state senator. It didn't move forward and died on Day 40, or Sine Die (meaning, "without a day"), the last day of the session.

I introduced and we passed another bill in the House that allowed only American citizens to sit on government boards, commissions, and authorities. If you have to be a citizen to vote, I thought it logical that only a citizen should be able to raise your taxes or fees. That was the next run-in I had with Stacey Abrams. She was on the House Rules Committee and tried to derail my bill and keep it off the House agenda. It passed and on it went to the Senate, but it, too, did not move forward and died on Day 40.

Another bill I introduced and passed stopped county tax commissioners from earning fees off the collection of delinquent property taxes. When a citizen is hurting financially, government employees shouldn't feast off their misfortune. That bill got solid bipartisan support in both chambers, and Governor Deal signed it into law.

After learning of hoax 911 calls, known as "swatting," that ended disastrously with innocent civilians or police killed, I introduced an anti-swatting bill to increase penalties. The bill was later incorporated into the governor's public safety bill that became law.

I also introduced and passed a bill that allowed business owners to renew their corporate charters for up to three years to reduce paperwork. Small business is the engine for job growth in America. As soon as I became secretary of state, I incorporated the three-year renewal option in our Corporations Division. There is great satisfaction when our office makes things just "a little bit better" for small business owners.

◆ ◆ ◆

In 2016, the state House majority whip Matt Ramsey from Peachtree City announced he would not be running for reelection. The majority whip and his team are responsible for taking a head count to gauge member support before major legislation comes to the floor. I looked around the House chamber and considered who might step up to replace him as whip, and I thought, *Why not me?*

I was in the middle of just my second legislative session, so I didn't have a lot of long-term connections.

The Republican caucus was showing signs of splintering over cultural issues. A major rift over a religious freedom bill, vetoed by Governor Deal, had left hurt feelings and raw nerves throughout the caucus. I believed I could help build bridges between the moderate and conservative wings of the party that might allow us to work together more effectively when contentious issues arose.

I expressed my interest to Speaker of the House David Ralston, and he pointed out my obvious weakness—my limited experience. He also believed a lawyer could be more effective in the role, even though our current speaker pro tem, Jan Jones—who was not a lawyer—had held that role earlier and did a superb job. I shared with the speaker my vision for building a unified caucus on a foundation of member input, consensus, and team loyalty, and he wished me well.

Over a period of months, I drove around the state and visited sixty House members in their businesses or at their favorite places for lunch. Most of them showed me around their hometowns and introduced me to local business leaders. I spoke to forty-five more Republican members by phone. Several other House members were running for majority whip—Trey Kelley, Chuck Efstration, and Christian Coomer—and I anticipated a friendly and respectful competition. They were lawyers, and I was not. I had built a successful business, and I knew how to build cohesive work teams and a successful organization. Each of us had particular strengths.

In early November, a week before the caucus meeting to elect officers, I visited the speaker and his chief of staff to catch them up with my travels across the state. The speaker listened, and we had what I thought was a cordial meeting.

Two nights later, John Pezold, a House member from Columbus, called me out of the blue. John and I were colleagues but weren't particularly close. He asked how the race for majority whip was going. I told him what I had shared with Speaker Ralston.

Then he said, "Brad, do you know that the speaker has cleared the field?"

"What are you talking about?" I asked.

"He's called everybody but you and told them to drop out. It's just you and Coomer."

Coomer was the speaker's man, but it wouldn't look good for him to run unopposed. He needed to defeat someone.

"He's setting you up, Brad," John said.

"I don't know," I said. "I was just in his office on Tuesday. If he wanted me out, he could have told me then."

"He's going to embarrass you," John said. "You don't toe the line."

"Let me think about it," I said, but when I hung up the phone the wind was completely out of my sails. I was astounded the speaker hadn't been more direct in our conversations. So was Tricia. Still, I didn't want to give up.

I called Sam Teasley, a representative from Marietta and vice chair of our caucus. He suggested, "You probably want to call a few more people and see where they stand, but I don't think it's going to happen for you. You won't have the votes." So I called and figured out that Sam and John were right.

I decided not to give the speaker the two-man race he wanted. Instead, I wrote a thank-you note to the caucus members, concluding, "Reflecting on your input and feedback and in light of other recent developments, I will not pursue a nomination for majority whip."

The experience made a mark with me. I had enjoyed traveling around the state and spending time with my fellow legislators outside the pressure and time constraints of the Capitol and the forty-day legislative session, and I began to think seriously about running for statewide office.

My other takeaway was that politics suffer when there is a lack of candor and honesty among politicians. Let your yes be yes and your no be no. Playing games behind people's backs seems so unproductive, and it does more than just embarrass the other person—it diminishes all the players in the game. Honesty and candor build trust.

In my business, I dealt with contractors every day. I was a contractor myself. I found that contractors shoot straight and have honest, direct conversations. We have to. Our work is right there for everybody to see and confirm. Our conversations may be high volume and include colorful language, but we resolve our problems and move forward to build and complete our projects on time and on budget. In the business world, we don't have time for games.

Secretary of State Brian Kemp was planning to run for governor in 2018, leaving that position open. As a legislator and a business owner, I had interacted often with different areas of the secretary of state's office. It touched on so many important and relevant aspects for all Georgians: honest and fair elections, corporation formation, professional licensing, securities, and charities. I saw it as a good fit for my strengths and interests.

Our son Kyle had been managing our business while I was at the Capitol during the legislative sessions, and he was ready to take over the company's day-to-day operations, allowing me to focus on a statewide run. If I won, I could dedicate myself full time to this new position. If I didn't win, I would know that I had made things a little bit better in the time that I served the people, and I would be content with that.

◆ ◆ ◆

During the 2018 legislative session, separate bills were introduced in the House and Senate to replace the aging voting machines we used statewide. Some legislators wanted to use paper ballots that voters would complete with a pen or pencil and feed into a scanner for tabulation. "The most secure system in the world for conducting elections is a pen or pencil and a piece of paper," Rep. Scot Turner said. Others favored a touch-screen machine that would generate a paper ballot that voters would review for accuracy and then scan.

Rep. Ed Setzler, sponsor of the House bill, suggested it was more important to move on from the old machines and not get bogged down in the details of the replacement at that time. "That's not the battle of the legislature," he said. "That's the battle of the town hall meetings. This is the venue to make a kind of muscle movement to get us to paper, then you guys are in the game and we get into rules and practices."

On the last day of the session, the House passed a substitute bill that the Senate disagreed with. Bottom line: neither bill became law. So in April 2018, the still-sitting Secretary of State, Brian Kemp, established the Secure, Accessible, and Fair Elections (SAFE) Commission to study the options and report to the legislature in 2019. He and Rep. Barry Fleming would cochair the commission.

We wrapped up the 2018 session at 12:20 a.m., Friday, March 28. Good Friday. While many around the world on Thursday had been remembering the Last Supper, we were busily passing the state budget, lowering the state income tax rate, increasing funding for charter schools, prohibiting people from handling their cell phones while driving, and much, much more.

I drove home, sad to be leaving my post in the House of Representatives but excited to begin my statewide campaign for secretary of state. Tricia and I would have the weekend together to celebrate Easter, and I would hit the road on Monday.

My message to voters needed to be clear and concise.

As an engineer, I thought about the "machinery" of elections—the process. What could we do to make the process more transparent, more accessible, more accurate, and ensure that it remained objectively fair?

At the same time, I thought about whether the results yielded by the election process were viewed subjectively by Georgians as trustworthy. Voters wanted to see for themselves that the process was fair. That meant ensuring the process was open.

The answers to both issues, transparency and trust, were paper ballots on Election Day and proper maintenance of the voter rolls, as required by Georgia law.

Georgians all agree that we should strive for voter rolls that are clean, up-to-date, and accurate. Georgians all agree that registration should be streamlined but maintain accuracy.

Three other Republicans were running for secretary of state: Sen. Josh McKoon from Columbus, Rep. Buzz Brockway from Gwinnett County, and former Alpharetta Mayor David Belle Isle.

The primary election was May 22. I had eight weeks to get my message out.

CHAPTER 4
UNQUESTIONED INTEGRITY

FOR KIDS STUDYING GEORGIA HISTORY, our most well-known secretary of state might be Ben Fortson. "Mr. Ben," as he was known, served in the position from 1947 until he died in 1979.

In his obituary, *The New York Times* wrote, "Mr. Fortson's integrity was unquestioned by even his adversaries during his thirty-four years in office, and fiscally conservative legislators routinely approved his budget requests while rejecting nearly everyone else's."[8]

What a legacy, and what an aspiration. His "integrity was unquestioned."

Any candidate running for office should aspire to that tribute.

I believe the secretary of state's position is less political and more procedural in nature. Where elections are concerned, the secretary of state acts as a neutral referee, never putting his or her thumb on one side of the scale or the other. A story about Ben Fortson illustrates this.

In 1946, Eugene Talmadge was elected as Georgia's governor but died before taking office. Melvin Thompson, who had been elected lieutenant governor, prodded the legislature to quickly certify the election results so he could step into the governor's place. But the legislature instead claimed it had the authority to select the next governor and chose Talmadge's son, Herman, to be governor. Governor Ellis Arnall, whose term was to end in January, refused to leave the office until the matter was settled. Then, overnight, Talmadge seized the office and had the locks changed.

In the midst of the "Three Governors Controversy," as it became known, was Secretary of State Fortson. He knew that the governor needed the official state seal to authenticate any official action taken by the governor. The seal was normally kept in a safe in the secretary of state's office at the capitol. For two months, while the courts determined the rightful governor, Mr. Ben hid the seal—under the cushion of his wheelchair!

The state supreme court ruled in March 1947 that Melvin Thompson was the rightful governor until a special election could be held. The state attorney general also ruled that any laws passed by the general assembly would be ruled unconstitutional until they were submitted to Thompson to approve or veto. Ben Fortson's decision to withhold the seal had been affirmed.

One bill passed by the legislature during that 1947 session and signed by Herman Talmadge—but never affixed with the official seal—would have created a "White Primary" for the Democratic Party. In an effort to bypass the U.S. Supreme Court's ruling that any primary election that excluded Black voters was unconstitutional, the legislature claimed the Democratic Party of Georgia was acting as a "political club" that sought to operate beyond the jurisdiction of federal courts. When Melvin Thompson officially took office, he vetoed the bill.

As a potential candidate for secretary of state, I had to take into account Georgia's history and the fact that for decades many of our citizens were denied the right to vote by earlier laws, poll taxes, "literacy" tests, and straight-up intimidation. If I won, I would be the secretary of state in Georgia, where Martin Luther King Jr. began the struggle for African-American voting rights. In that context, I understood that this was a visceral, deep issue for a huge portion of the state population who had been denied the right to freely vote. So I was committed to honest and fair elections with unquestioned integrity that are open and accessible to every legal voter.

At this juncture in our lives, real tragedy hit home. On the evening of April 3, 2018, we were told over the phone by the city of Atlanta Police Department that Brenton, our oldest son, had died from an overdose of fentanyl. As I said earlier, it is the worst news a parent can receive. It doesn't matter how old your child is or what they died from, the loss is overwhelming.

After several weeks, I went back out on the campaign trail, which served as a distraction for me while I grieved. Driving across the great state of Georgia allowed me plenty of time to process, assess, and grieve. Brenton loved politics, and he was one of my biggest cheerleaders in the political arena. I knew he would want me to continue. We still miss him, and we always will.

◆ ◆ ◆

Every politician has a stump speech, and mine went something like this:

As an engineer, I think about the machinery of elections. I think about the process. What can we do to make the process more transparent? What can we do to make the process more accessible, more accurate, and make sure the process is objectively fair?

I think about whether Georgians subjectively trust the results of that process.

To trust an election, they must see that the process is fair. So we must ensure the process is open.

Georgians all agree that we should strive for voter rolls that are clean, up-to-date, and accurate. Georgians all agree that registration should be streamlined but maintain accuracy.

Accuracy is not suppression when it is applied with Wisdom, Justice, and Moderation [our state motto]. *Voter protection is not discrimination when it is applied with Wisdom, Justice, and Moderation. Up-to-date and accurate voter rolls are not the enemy of participation when applied with Wisdom, Justice, and Moderation.*

As we change over to new voting machines, Georgia has a once-in-a-lifetime opportunity to create a process that is objectively fair and yields an outcome that Georgians, individually and as a whole, subjectively trust.

I also spoke of updates to the less well-known responsibilities of the secretary of state's office: corporations, professional license boards, and securities.

In the primary, I finished first among four Republicans with 35 percent of the votes. Two months later, I won the runoff with just under 62 percent of the votes.

In the general election, my opponents were former Democratic Congressman John Barrow and Libertarian Smythe Duval.

Barrow had an interesting career in Congress, serving five terms from the 12th District. His district had been added to Georgia after the 2000 census, when Democrats were in control of the legislature. He won the seat in 2004, and later, when Republicans had control of the Senate and House, they redrew the district boundaries so that he no longer lived in his own district. When he moved from Athens to Savannah and won again, Republicans carved him out a second time. So he moved to Augusta and won again. Finally, in 2014, Barrow lost to Republican Rick Allen.

All those boundary changes gave Barrow an advantage in a statewide race against me because of his name recognition across dozens of counties where he had campaigned for a decade. He was the former congressman from *everywhere*.

My name recognition, on the other hand, was not so great. *The New York Times* referred to me as "Ben Raffensperger," and in another article, the *Times* described me as "long on intelligence and short on charisma."[9]

Okay. I'll accept that. But Georgia voters twice elected a governor whose campaign slogan was, "A workhorse, not a showhorse."

I finished first in the three-way race with 49 percent of the vote, which meant I'd have to face Barrow again in a runoff election four weeks later.

Barrow was a lawyer and an excellent speaker, quick on his feet. I understood my limitations. I'm an engineer. I had to present a message that resonated with a majority of the voters. In an op-ed column for *The Atlanta Journal-Constitution*, I invoked the name of Primus King, a Black man in Muscogee County who had attempted to vote in a Democratic primary held on Independence Day 1944. Since 1908, Georgia had allowed white-only party primaries, and because Georgia was virtually a one-party state (Democrat), exclusion from the primary meant exclusion from the franchise altogether.

King was prevented from voting and tossed into the street. His attorney promptly filed a lawsuit against the Muscogee County Democratic Party. A judge ruled in King's favor, and the appeals courts upheld the decision.

In my op-ed, I wrote:

Regretfully, Georgia's past is stained with similar injustices.

As I think about the role of the Secretary of State as Georgia's Chief Election Officer, I step back from the passions and overheated partisan rhetoric of a hotly contested election. . . .

It is through voting that we actually live the proposition that we are all equal. Every registered voter gets one vote. Bill Gates gets one vote. The nineteen-year-old college student gets one vote. And thus we reaffirm, as regularly and as often as every election season, the idea that makes us one. We are all equal before the law. We all count. We all have a voice. . . .

My view is that this election is about using this unique and historic opportunity to create a voting system that is modern, efficient, accurate, secure, safe, verifiable, fair, accessible, and trustworthy.

As your secretary of state, I promise to you that I will devote myself to creating a system that would be worthy of patriots like Primus King.[10]

As the campaign neared its end, we scheduled a bus tour across the state, and Tricia felt she was ready to join me. Tricia has always been supportive of my interest in politics, though it hasn't been one of her favorite things to do. Photography had been her hobby for about six years at that point. So between grieving for our son and finding comfort in spending her time photographing, she had not been on the trail with me often. Tricia had not met many of the Georgians with whom I had been spending time over the last six months.

She experienced firsthand the wonderful South Georgia hospitality I had been telling her about and got a small glimpse of why I wanted to serve this great state as the secretary of state. She saw my passion to serve and was excited at that prospect.

It was a great week traveling on the whistle-stop tour, building excitement and momentum for the runoff.

On December 4, 2018, I was elected in the runoff with 51.9 percent of the vote.

Although Republicans won every statewide office in Georgia that year, the competitive election results for nearly every statewide office provided a clear indication that, although Georgia was still a red state, the Democrats were making inroads.

In fact, our state was changing faster than many Republicans were willing to admit.

◆ ◆ ◆

Brian Kemp had been elected governor in November. He resigned as secretary of state to prepare for his new role, and Governor Deal appointed Robyn Crittenden to fill Kemp's unexpired term. She joined Rep. Barry Fleming as cochair of the Secure, Accessible, and Fair Elections (SAFE) Commission, which included Republican and Democratic legislators as well as the general counsels from the Republican and Democratic Parties of Georgia and from the executive committee of the Libertarian Party of Georgia. Election officials from five counties also served on the commission, as did the co-executive director of Georgia Tech's Institute for Information Security and Privacy. I was also a member of the committee.

We reached out to voting machine vendors with a request for information (RFI) on our options to replace Georgia's voting machines, electronic poll book system, election management software, precinct scanners and tabulators, and election night reporting website. Seven vendors responded.

I invited former Secretary of State Cathy Cox to the December meeting, and she described the history of the state of our voting technology leading up to the turn of the twenty-first century. In decades past, Georgia counties had bought their own voting machines. By the end of the twentieth century, several counties were still using voting booths that hadn't been manufactured in half a century. If you're as old as I am, you may remember them. You stepped in and pushed a big lever that closed a curtain behind you. You flipped a small lever for each of your candidates, then pulled the big lever to register your votes and open the curtain. Jurisdictions across the country used the machines throughout the twentieth century, even though there was no paper ballot, meaning no audit trail.

Other Georgia counties were using the same type punch cards that Florida had in 2000. Remember "hanging chads"?

Still, others used optical scanners for paper ballots with "bubbles" for voters to fill in. For younger voters who had grown up with standardized tests, the ballots were intuitive. They were not so easy for all, however. Some voters drew a circle around the candidate's name, and others wrote an X out to the side of their candidate's name. None of those votes would be recognized by the scanner.

Finally, two counties were using "bed-sheet-size" paper ballots that were marked and counted by hand.

In the 2000 Bush-Gore presidential election, 94,000 Georgians' ballots did not include a vote for any presidential candidate or included votes for more than one. That was 3.5 percent of all Georgia ballots—more than Florida's 2.9 percent and twice the national average. The counties with the highest error rate were those with optical scanners and paper ballots.

George W. Bush won Georgia by more than 300,000 votes, so we didn't have the same problems Florida had in 2000. But Georgia still had a problem.

After the 2000 election, the assumption was that "paper is bad!" and "electronics are great!" Electronic equipment ensured voters would vote only once in each race, and the machines reminded voters if they had not yet voted in a particular race, giving more clarity to voters and for tabulating. They were also more accessible for voters with disabilities.

Cathy Cox led the state to a twenty-first-century solution, and Georgia became the first state to move to all-electronic voting machines. Through the Help America Vote Act (HAVA), Georgia was able to procure federal grants to purchase 19,000 direct-recording electronic (DRE) machines—enough for all 159 counties.

Voters inserted a card with a magnetic strip, like a credit card, into the machine and then made their choices on a touch screen. The card told the machine what ballot the voter should get. When a voter finished voting, they touched a button entitled "Cast Ballot," and their selections were directly recorded onto a memory card contained in the voting machine. At the close of voting, each machine printed a strip of paper containing the vote tallies and county election officials uploaded the memory cards into a central server in each county.

The DREs were not without their detractors. A small group, mostly Republicans, voiced concerns that electronics could not be trusted. The new machines did not print a paper ballot for the voter to review and submit, and without paper there was no way to conduct a hand recount or an audit in the case of a close race. All the information was electronic, stored on the memory cards and in the computers.

Then Republican Sonny Perdue upset the Democratic incumbent in 2002, and two years later Republicans controlled the Georgia House and Senate. As a result, concerns from the right about electronic voting machines mostly subsided. But the issue never disappeared.

By 2006, Secretary of State Cox had joined the voices of those concerned by the lack of physical evidence of the voter's choice. "We are actively exploring options to modify and enhance Georgia's voting system," she said in a formal statement to media, "to provide a voter-verified paper trail that gives voters even more confidence in our voting process."

It never happened. Thirteen years later, in January 2019, the SAFE Commission recommended:

1. Georgia should adopt a voting system with a verifiable paper vote record. Every effort should be made to implement this system statewide in time for the 2020 election. The system should create an auditable paper record for every vote that the voter has an opportunity to review before casting. Rules should be put in place ensuring a rigorous chain of custody for these paper records, as are in place now for security of paper ballots and memory cards.

The Commission unanimously agrees that Georgia should move to a new voting system that provides a verifiable paper vote record. . . . The Commission further unanimously agrees that Georgia should make every effort to implement this system in time for the 2020 election cycle.

A verifiable paper vote record is a method of providing feedback to voters using a paper ballot that is either marked by hand or on a ballot-marking device with a verifiable paper ballot.

Voter's choices are either marked by hand with a writing utensil or marked on a screen in a similar manner to a DRE [direct-recording electronic device] on a tablet device. However, a ballot-marking device with a verifiable paper ballot does not record the voter's choices into its memory. Instead, it allows the voter to mark the choices on-screen and, when the voter is done, prints the ballot selections in a manner that allows the voter to easily read their selections. The resulting printed paper ballot is then counted using a digital scanner and tabulator. This printed paper ballot, which is the official ballot, is then fed through a scanner into a locked ballot box so that all originals are saved for auditing and recounts. Additionally, the voter has the ability to proofread the ballot before it is scanned and have it voided and start over if there is an error.

2. *Georgia should remain a uniform system state, with each county using the same equipment that is initially provided by the state.*

Georgia currently utilizes a uniform election system, meaning that every county in Georgia uses the same type of DREs, electronic poll books, and the same Election Management System. The SAFE Commission recommends that Georgia remain uniform in its next system.

3. *The implementation of a new system should include a training plan and budget to educate both voters and county election officials.*

The SAFE Commission recognizes the importance of both voter education and election official training as we move to a new system, and the Commission recommends that the state take a similar approach to training and education during this implementation as it did during the implementation of the current system.

4. *Any new system should ensure that disabled voters have the same opportunity for access and participation as other voters in accordance with the Help Americans Vote Act and the Americans with Disabilities Act. Any new system should be certified by the Election Assistance Commission.*

5. *Georgia's new voting system should include new vote casting devices, new scanners, and new poll books. There should be paper backups for each of these systems to the extent possible, including paper registered voter lists and ballots. For each new type of hardware, steps should be taken to ensure both security and functionality. Any new hardware or software needs to be compatible with Georgia's existing voter registration system.*

While much of the attention regarding voting systems revolves around the vote casting devices, there is a host of other equipment that is vital to administering secure, accessible, and fair elections.

As with any piece of hardware or software, security must be a top priority. As SAFE Commission member Dr. Wenke Lee has pointed out, "even when a system is not directly connected to the Internet it can still be attacked by those who have direct access or via data that can be traced back to an Internet facing system." In order to ensure a high level of security of voting system components, Georgia should adopt security rules based on the following guidelines. Georgia should also ensure that any technology that touches any aspect of a voting system is secure. These recommendations are more appropriate for promulgation by the State Election Board as administrative rules rather than being adopted in statute. These steps include but are not limited to:

- Restricting device functionality to only what is required (e.g., disabling Wi-Fi, Bluetooth, or Internet connectivity when not needed for updates or specific functionality).
- Physically disable or otherwise seal exposed ports.
- Encrypt any data transmissions.
- Conduct regular penetration testing.
- Treat all removable media as potential delivery mechanism for malware and put in place appropriate policies for the use of removable media (e.g., thumb drives, etc.).
- Ensure that there is a consistent process to securely patch and update software on devices.
- For any vendor that provides hardware or software—require vendor security measures in accordance with industry best practices, such as those established by the National Institute of Standards and Technology. Such security requirements for any potential vendor should be included in the RFP (request for proposal) process and in any contract so that vendors hold responsibility for cybersecurity failures and are incentivized to properly maintain equipment under contract.
- Have an ability to "hash-test" software to ensure that the code on the hardware matches the certified source code.

6. *Given Georgia's history as a state that uses DREs and the familiarity of voters and election officials with that method of vote casting, Georgia should move to a primarily ballot-marking device with verifiable paper ballots solution for a new voting system.*

While all other recommendations of the SAFE Commission represent the unanimous view of the Commission, the Commission was not able to come to a unanimous view on how Georgia voters should mark their ballots on Georgia's next voting system. A majority of the Commission believes that Georgia should utilize ballot-marking devices with verifiable paper ballots as the in-person method of voting for Georgia's next voting system. . . . The Commission believes that ballot-marking devices provide clearer voter intent and that moving from one form of touchscreen voting to another will be an easier transition for Georgia voters than it would be to move to hand-marked paper ballots.

SAFE Commission member Dr. Wenke Lee, Professor of Computer Science in the College of Computing at the Georgia Institution for Technology, who also holds the John P. Imlay Chair in Software at Georgia Tech, strongly feels that hand-marked paper ballots are more secure than ballots marked using ballot-marking devices. This view is also held and was expressed to the Commission by Verified Voting and numerous professors in computer science and cybersecurity. . . . Dr. Lee's concern with ballot-marking devices with verifiable paper ballots is that there is not a systemic study that shows that voters actually do verify their ballot selection even when they have the opportunity. He is also concerned that even voters who attempt to verify their selections may not actually remember them.

The voting systems demonstrated to the Commission use either bar codes, QR codes, or optical character recognition (OCR) in order to tabulate marked ballots. The Commission reiterates its recommendation that the paper ballot that is generated in Georgia's next voting system must allow the voter to verify his or her selections and cure any errors prior to scanning the ballot.

Additionally, Georgia law should be updated to clarify that the human readable component of the ballot is the official vote record.

> **7. Georgia should require post-election, pre-certification audits. These audits will certainly be time consuming and add work to county election officials, but they are necessary to show transparency and maintain trust in the elections process.**

The Commission recognizes that this requirement adds another post-Election Day activity to county election officials, and recommends that the General Assembly consider amended post-election deadlines for certification to ensure that an audit can be conducted without lengthening the overall certification process. The Commission recommends that the General Assembly put in place an audit requirement for all elections from the November 2020 election going forward, but recommends that the General Assembly not require a certain type of audit, instead leaving the specifics to the State Election Board to enact via administrative rule so that Georgia can be more responsive to updates in election auditing.

> **8. In order to successfully implement this new system, other areas of Georgia election law should be updated to ensure compatibility with the new system and improve election administration. Some of these updates may require updates to Georgia statutes, while some may be better suited to regulations promulgated by the State Election Board.[11]**

Implementing the bipartisan SAFE Commission's recommendations would create a voting system with integrity Georgia voters could trust—a verifiable paper vote record, an auditable paper record for every vote, a rigorous chain of custody for ballots and records, and post-election audits. Planning all this was a phenomenal effort by everyone involved. But as we'd soon find out, the hard work—not to mention the national scrutiny—was just beginning.

CHAPTER 5
CYNICAL, POLL-TESTED STRATEGIES

CERTAIN TERMS ARE LIGHTNING RODS FOR animating large groups of people and urging them to act. One of those is the phrase "voter suppression." Around 2014, Stacey Abrams began working to put Democrats in charge in Georgia, with her intermediate goal of becoming governor and her long-term goal of becoming president.

Her strategy was simple: to neutralize all Republican opposition, just allege "voter suppression" whenever Republicans talk about voter integrity and ballot security. If Republicans want to outlaw absentee-ballot harvesting, just say that's voter suppression. If Republicans conduct routine voter list maintenance to keep the voter rolls accurate, as required by the federal National Voter Registration Act, assert such action is nothing less than voter suppression.

Much like the tonic of the traveling salesman of bygone years, her response to every issue is "voter suppression." It works because it touches the sensitive third rail of politics—voting rights. I get that. Georgia, like the rest of the South and indeed our nation, has a troubled history concerning equal treatment and opportunity for Black Americans. My problem with Stacey Abrams is the same problem many people have with Donald Trump.

Let me explain.

The media often use terms such as "grievance politics" or "politics of resentment" to describe President Trump's style. He tells his voters that they should be angry. They're not getting what they deserve—their "fair share."

In 2016, political scientist Katherine J. Cramer, author of *The Politics of Resentment*, told *Scientific American* magazine, "What I heard [Donald Trump] saying was: You are right, you are not getting your fair share, you should be angry, you are a deserving, hardworking American and what you deserve is going to people who don't deserve it."[12]

Trump turned that anger into victory in 2016. Four years later, he claimed the election wasn't just stolen from him, it was stolen from his voters.

Similarly, Abrams turned anger at perceived voter suppression into certain people not accepting the results of a tight race between herself and Brian Kemp in the 2018 gubernatorial election. But as with Trump, her claim was not supported by the truth, and it divides us unnecessarily on artificial issues.

As I write these words, I understand that the voting rights topic requires immense sensitivity with our words and actions, perhaps more sensitivity than my words can communicate. It was only in 1965 that the Voting Rights Act was passed in Congress. Much has improved, and America is better for it. But we are not yet finished. I understand that. In a perfect world, every adult American citizen who wants to vote would have easy access to the polls, and every vote cast would be a legal vote.

I believe a political party's message should attract 50 percent plus one vote to elect candidates. If our message doesn't, we should change our message.

It turns out that "voter suppression" was a planned-for strategy. In 2019, Voter Access Institute (VAI) founder Lauren Groh-Wargo, by then Stacey Abrams's campaign manager and chief executive of VAI's successor organization, Fair Fight Action, said the VAI had poll-tested "voter suppression" as a get-out-the-vote strategy as early as 2014. In a sworn deposition Groh-Wargo said the institute conducted a poll that year "with unregistered and low-propensity African-Americans and Latinos around why voting matters, using themes of voter suppression."[13] The timing of this poll suggests that years before alleging the 2018 gubernatorial election had been stolen from her, Abrams and her team had already determined that claims of voter suppression would make a powerful political strategy.

Those same claims, however, were not so effective in courtrooms, where actual evidence has to be presented.

◆ ◆ ◆

Background: The National Voter Registration Act (NVRA) of 1993, which "requires States to implement procedures to maintain accurate and current voter registration lists," was passed by a Democratic U.S. House and Senate and signed into law by President Bill Clinton. To adhere to the federal law, the 1994 Georgia General Assembly, led by Democrats, passed a law requiring voter roll maintenance. Governor Zell Miller, also a Democrat, signed into law the bill that required election officials to remove individuals from the voter rolls if they (1) have not interacted with election officials in three years, (2) have not responded to a postcard sent to their listed address, and (3) failed to vote in the two subsequent general elections.

A quarter of a century later, this law and its implementation lay at the heart of multiple lawsuits filed by Common Cause, the NAACP, Fair Fight, and others.

Spoiler alert: Despite the talking points and the headlines that led many to believe otherwise, the federal courts found that Georgia's list maintenance process complies with the NVRA. Georgia's process is similar to Ohio's, and Ohio's law was upheld in 2018 by the U.S. Supreme Court. After that decision, the plaintiffs in Georgia voluntarily dismissed their case. A later lawsuit by Fair Fight raised similar issues, and the court in that case also ruled in Georgia's favor.

◆ ◆ ◆

When I took office as secretary of state, at least nine court cases were pending that had been filed by liberal groups seeking to challenge or undermine confidence in the result of the 2018 gubernatorial election in Georgia. The claims ranged from the simply inaccurate to the truly preposterous. We have been able to successfully defend Georgia law in each of those cases.

Sarah Riggs Amico, the Democratic nominee for lieutenant governor, supported an election contest filed by a group called the Coalition for Good Governance, whose largest funder is Stacey Abrams's Fair Fight, alleging that she lost her race because voting machines "lost" 100,000 votes. The judge correctly rejected her claim, but it was treated with abject seriousness by the liberal media (similar to how right-wing media would treat similar claims brought by President Trump's allies following the 2020 election).

The Brennan Center for Justice, a liberal group from New York University Law School, brought a case alleging "malfeasance or tampering with Georgia's voter registration database," that an "attacker can change or cancel voter registrations," and there is "no way to know how many voters may have been affected." In court in that case, Myrna Perez, head of the Brennan Center's Voting Rights and Elections Program said, "It is our worry that Putin or some other criminal was messing with the voter registration database and messing up the registrations so that it wrongfully and improperly indicated they were not eligible to vote."[14] Just like President Trump and his allies two years later, they did not present any evidence that any of their allegations had actually occurred. But the unsupported, sensationalized claims were repeated with gusto by a sympathetic media.

The main source cited in this complaint was a liberal blog post based on an election-eve political attack from the Democratic Party of Georgia. Fortunately, even a liberal judge sympathetic to the Brennan Center's position declined to grant the relief they asked for, which was to accept provisional ballots that had been cast by unregistered voters. The Brennan Center's complaint was ridiculous, but it foreshadowed a strategy that would later be employed by allies of President Trump following the 2020 election—allege that something bad may have happened even if you are not sure it did and have no evidence that it did, then run to court saying that the U.S. Constitution requires the court to step in and overturn the results of the election.

Another case, brought by the Lawyer's Committee for Civil Rights (whose then-president, Kristen Clarke, now leads the Civil Rights Division of the Department of Justice under President Biden), asked a court to order ballots cast by people who had been identified as non-citizens by Georgia's Department of Driver Services to be counted with no further action from the voter. (Georgia law allows those voters to either show their proof of citizenship at the polls or cast a provisional ballot and show their proof of citizenship to their county registrar within three days after the election.) After conservative groups hammered the complaint for seeking to allow non-citizens to vote, the Lawyer's Committee amended their complaint to clarify that they were only asking to count those ballots after the voter had shown proof of citizenship, which was already the law in Georgia.

Fortunately, the judge declined to grant them the relief they asked for and ordered only a minor change in Georgia's process that kept the citizenship check in place.

With the liberal Brennan Center asking a court to order Georgia to count votes from unregistered voters and the liberal Lawyer's Committee asking a court to order Georgia to count votes from potential non-citizens, is it any wonder that conservatives accuse liberals of seeking to let ineligible voters vote? The shoe seems to fit. Fortunately, our office was able to successfully defend Georgia law in each of these cases.

Perhaps the best-known lawsuit following the 2018 election was the one brought by Stacey Abrams following her loss by 55,000 votes in the gubernatorial election. On November 16, 2018, she refused to concede that she lost the election and said, "In the coming days, we will be filing a major federal lawsuit against the State of Georgia." Rudy Guiliani would say the same thing almost exactly two years later. The lawsuit, like Abrams's speech, attracted massive nationwide media attention.

Whether by coincidence or by design, a pattern soon emerged.

- Make public charges and file a headline-generating federal lawsuit.
- Repeat incendiary talking points.
- Raise money.

Abrams founded the group Fair Fight to file this lawsuit. The lawsuit made a media splash when it was filed, helped to raise Abrams's profile, and led to millions of dollars in donations. Again, in eerily similar language to what supporters of President Trump would say following the 2020 election, Fair Fight alleged that Georgia citizens had been "denied the ability to elect their leaders" and stated that Georgia's voting system was "virtually guaranteed to fail." Matching their ideological friends from the Brennan Center, they alleged that the system was "vulnerable to hacking" but did not allege that any hacking had actually occurred. They also alleged, again foreshadowing what President Trump and his allies would allege two years later, that machines had "flipped votes."

While Fair Fight's complaint used the same over-the-top and false rhetoric that Abrams's campaign utilized, their actual legal claims fell far short of the scorching accusations she leveled at my predecessor. Abrams accused then Secretary Kemp of being an "architect of voter suppression," but the actual laws and practices she challenged were long-standing laws whose execution had not significantly changed under secretaries of state of either party. And the "evidence" that she used to support her claims, again foreshadowing what Trump allies would do following the 2020 election, consisted of hastily gathering declarations from political supporters that would proceed to fall apart under further investigation.

One voter submitted a declaration stating that he never received his absentee ballot, then admitted during his deposition that he had received his ballot but wanted to vote in person instead. Another claimant did have trouble obtaining an absentee ballot, but once he received one, he refused to believe the election system's claim that his ballot had been accepted. A third witness was frustrated that she had to vote provisionally at her assigned polling location, but she left out of her declaration the fact that the election system had ultimately accepted her provisional ballot. In short, the alleged reams of disenfranchised voters largely amounted to people who were confused about the rules or had misrepresented their situations. In some cases, the witnesses acknowledged they had submitted a declaration to help Abrams. Some even admitted to not having written their own declarations.

Regarding their actual legal claims, the voting machines that Fair Fight complained of were brought to Georgia by a Democratic secretary of state with a law passed by a Democratic general assembly and signed by a Democratic governor. Fair Fight ignominiously dropped their claims of "vote flipping" or other machine issues before the judge could issue any sort of ruling on them (in yet another move that President Trump would copy two years later—dismissing his election contest on the eve of trial and avoiding a judicial ruling on the subject).

Fair Fights' claims over what they call "voter purges"—but should be more accurately called "voter list maintenance"—follow the same pattern. They sued over a law that was passed by a Democratic general assembly and signed by a Democratic governor. And while the number of voters removed increased in recent years, that's because of the overall increase in registered voters due to population growth, implementation of online voter registration, and implementation of automatic voter registration (both of which occurred during my Republican predecessor's administration).

Fair Fight also sued over a long-standing state law implementing a required portion of the federal Help America Vote Act. HAVA requires that states match new voter registrants' information submitted on their voter registration with their existing information on file at the state department of motor vehicles (Department of Driver Services in Georgia). Fair Fight misleadingly calls this "exact match." They leave out that it is a federally mandated policy and that any voter who does not match can "cure" the failure simply by showing their ID at the polls (which is what every Georgia voter has to do before they can vote). I never understood how requiring the same thing of these voters as Georgia requires of every voter supported the rhetoric that these voter registrations were "held up."

As the case progressed, it became clearer and clearer that the rhetoric Abrams and her allies employed during her campaign did not come close to matching the reality of Georgia's election law and processes. In February 2021, United States District Judge Steve Jones issued an order that found that on almost all of Fair

Fight's claims, they had not shown the small amount of evidence that would allow them to proceed to a trial. Even if some of Fair Fight's claims do eventually proceed to trial (and I am confident that the state will prevail if any do), the record of actual evidence shows that Abrams's and her allies' political rhetoric was false and misleading.

I have been defending Georgia's election laws and practices from false and specious claims from the moment I was sworn in as secretary of state, and I knew I would be doing the same thing in the lead-up to and following the 2020 election. But I had no idea I would be going up against our nation's highest officeholder.

DONALD TRUMP ATTACKS

Below are a series of tweets from President Trump immediately following the presidential election. The 2012 presidential election.

> This election is a total sham and a travesty. We are not a democracy!
> — Donald J. Trump (@realDonaldTrump)[15]

> More votes equals a loss . . . revolution!
> — Donald J. Trump (@realDonaldTrump)[16]

> We can't let this happen. We should march on Washington and stop this travesty. Our nation is totally divided!
> — Donald J. Trump (@realDonaldTrump)[17]

> Lets fight like hell and stop this great and disgusting injustice! The world is laughing at us.
> — Donald J. Trump (@realDonaldTrump)[18]

Trump tweeted these statements on November 6, 2012, when it appeared Republican candidate Mitt Romney would receive more popular votes but lose in the Electoral College vote. (As it turned out, Barack Obama received about 5 million more votes than Romney.)

When Trump was trailing in the polls prior to the 2016 presidential election, he again attacked our voting system, despite there being no evidence of widespread voter fraud. On August 1, 2016, he told a crowd in Columbus, Ohio, "I'm afraid the election is going to be rigged, I'm going to be honest."

This pattern of evidence-free attacks on our system had a concrete impact on Americans' trust in our democracy. Even before the 2016 election, large numbers of Trump supporters said they believed the election could be stolen from him. House Speaker Paul Ryan was concerned enough by Trump's rhetoric to have his spokesperson release a statement in response: "Our democracy relies on confidence in election results, and the speaker is fully confident the states will carry out this election with integrity."[19]

Democrats and the media condemned Trump's false claims.

Then came Georgia's 2018 gubernatorial election in which Democrat Stacey Abrams lost to Republican Brian Kemp by 54,723 votes. Almost immediately you would have thought Donald Trump had written the cue cards for Abrams and her supporters.

Washington Post senior political reporter Aaron Blake noticed right away, and wrote an analysis with the headline: "Democrats are now going there on 'stolen' elections":

> *And now even some big-name Democrats are using similar language, alleging that the Georgia governor's race will be "stolen" from them, too. . . .*

> *. . . they could merely argue that the courts need to intervene or that Kemp's apparent win would have a cloud hanging over it; instead, they are declaring it invalid. Practically speaking, they are alleging illegal activity that hasn't been proven—and seems unlikely to be. . . .*

However you feel about the underlying issues, saying the election is being stolen skips over all of that and can't help but undermine confidence in American elections. Democrats might say it deserves to be undermined, given [their allegations], but it's a very serious accusation that has implications for our entire political and legal system. If leaders of both parties are alleging this kind of thing is possible in huge races in neighboring states and implying that legal remedies are insufficient to stop it, that's a recipe for widespread mistrust of elections.[20]

Among those claiming that the election had been "stolen" from Stacey Abrams were a veritable who's who of Democratic politicians:

"I think that Stacey Abrams's election is being stolen from her, using what I think are insidious measures to disenfranchise certain groups of people. . . . To me, it's the appearance of voter fraud, voter disenfranchisement, voter suppression."

— *Senator Cory Booker, November 13, 2018*[21]

"If she had a fair election, she already would have won."

— *Former Secretary of State Hillary Clinton, November 13, 2018*[22]

"If Stacey Abrams doesn't win in Georgia, they stole it."

— *Senator Sherrod Brown, November 14, 2018*[23]

On November 16, 2018, ten days after Election Day, Stacey Abrams told a crowd of her supporters, "So to be clear, this is not a speech of concession. Concession means to acknowledge an action is right, true or proper. As a woman of conscience and faith, I cannot concede."[24] As of the writing of this book, Stacey Abrams has still not conceded the 2018 gubernatorial election.

Mainstream news outlets were soon echoing allegations from Abrams and her allies. At first, these focused on conflict-of-interest accusations against Abrams's opponent, Brian Kemp—my predecessor as Georgia's secretary of state. Secretaries of state regularly run for reelection, of course, and previous secretaries of state in Georgia had run for governor without eliciting controversy.

The stolen-election narrative started to take hold, and the NAACP proclaimed that "Kemp's actions during the election were textbook voter suppression,"[25] while *Rolling Stone* declared that judges were "doing all they [could] to keep Brian Kemp from stealing the Georgia election."[26] Citing an Emory University professor who described these alleged efforts as "Jim Crow 2.0," *The Atlantic* opined that "the Georgia governor's race [had] brought voter suppression into full view."[27] Only after the 2020 election did the mainstream media started to realize the error of their ways, with Nate Cohn of *The New York Times* recently stating, "Georgia voting law has long been a lot closer to the national average than the critics acknowledge."[28]

Despite the absence of evidence, the notion that Kemp stole the election from Abrams became an article of faith among the Democratic Party leadership. Senator Bernie Sanders soon followed suit, arguing during a Georgia presidential debate that "voter suppression . . . [had] cost the Democratic Party a governorship."[29] In June 2019, then-presidential candidate Joe Biden claimed that "voter suppression is the reason Stacey Abrams isn't governor right now."[30] Former Democratic presidential nominee Hillary Clinton also chimed in, as did Sen. Kamala Harris, who insisted that "without voter suppression, Stacey Abrams would be the governor of Georgia."[31]

Given the continued inflammatory and false rhetoric from liberal politicians regarding Georgia's elections, I knew that Georgia would be even more in the liberal litigation crosshairs in the lead-up to the 2020 election. Our office, along with the Georgia attorney general, defended the state against these lawsuits and others that followed, but the state simply did not have even close to the amount of resources that the liberal activist groups and their big-law attorney allies brought to these cases. They absorbed precious manpower resources and significant state budget dollars for legal costs. We needed help, so several of my senior staff and I traveled to Washington, D.C., to meet with conservative think tanks and the Republican National Committee. We told the RNC, The Heritage Foundation, Judicial Watch, and the American Constitutional Rights Union what conservatives were facing in Georgia. I asked what resources they could dedicate for filing briefs or providing peer-reviewed research to help us with this litigation onslaught.

They politely told us there was no funding for any of this. Election integrity wasn't something that Republicans, or by extension then-sitting President Donald J. Trump, saw the value in defending in the lead up to the 2020 election. We knew that Georgia would be a major target of Democratic election litigation in 2020, and it was up to us and the state attorney general to defend Georgia's laws.

In the meantime, Fair Fight became a juggernaut of fundraising and political organizing. According to the Georgia's Government Transparency and Campaign Finance Commission, Fair Fight raised almost $90 million and spent at least $66 million during the 2019–2020 election cycle. During the two-month lead-up to the U.S. Senate runoff elections in Georgia the PAC raised $22.3 million, which it put toward securing victories for Democratic candidates Jon Ossoff and Raphael Warnock.[32]

One of Fair Fight's main voter-suppression claims involved the closing of polling places. Abrams, Fair Fight, and their allies alleged that, since the 2013 Supreme Court ruling in *Shelby County v. Holder* (which effectively removed federal preclearance requirements for voting changes in Georgia and other jurisdictions), Republican officials have been closing polling locations around the state to disproportionately harm minority voters. My predecessor and I have often been cast as the villains in this tale.

But there has always been one major flaw in this theory: the state government and the secretary of state have no authority over polling places. Under Georgia law, decisions concerning polling places are made at the county level. Abrams and her allies know this. In their complaint, they acknowledge, "Georgia counties have responsibility for some aspects of Georgia elections," but they gloss over the fact that the local-control structure of election administration applies to polling-place locations. Instead, they vaguely allege that "the Secretary . . . served as Georgia's chief architect of [the] voting barriers."[33]

Allegations of voter "purges" also appear in Fair Fight's legal filings. These charges mirror those raised in Abrams's November 2018 non-concession speech, in which she claimed that "more than a million citizens found their names stripped from the rolls by the Secretary of State" while "tens of thousands" more "hung in limbo," their votes "rejected due to human error and a system of suppression that had already proven its bias."[34] The filings neglect to mention that both state and federal law require the secretary of state's office to review voter rolls to ensure that the information is both accurate and up to date, that the courts upheld this practice in 2019, and that states such as Nevada, Illinois, Colorado, and Maryland have all experienced similar reductions in the sizes of their voter lists due in part to similar voter-roll maintenance policies.

If my predecessor and I had improperly removed a million voters from the rolls, there would have been a widespread outcry among the voters themselves. But that hasn't happened. One local reporter knocked on the doors of thirty individuals scheduled for removal from the voter rolls to investigate the voter-purge claim. At those addresses he found deceased voters, abandoned homes, and empty lots.

Abrams and her allies made the fiction that Republican officials had suppressed votes to steal her election a cornerstone of their post-election political and fundraising strategy.

Additional lawsuits would follow shortly.

CHAPTER 6
BUILDING A MORE SECURE VOTING SYSTEM

I TOOK OFFICE ON JANUARY 14, 2019, with fourteen months to prepare for a presidential primary and no voting machines. Everybody understood the need to move quickly.

We were in a mad dash from day one. Our first priority was to get authorization and direction from the General Assembly, which was in session, to purchase new equipment.

My staff and I hoped we would find a request for proposal (RFP) for voting machines prepared by the outgoing secretary of state staff awaiting us when we took office. We did not. They had put out a request for information, and the responses from seven voting machine manufacturers gave us a starting point to draft an RFP.

I had been elected secretary of state by voters using sixteen-year-old touch-screen voting machines. Georgia was one of only five states using direct-recording electronic (DRE) voting machines, and with mounting concerns of potential foreign and domestic attempts to hack and alter the results of American elections, Georgia moved toward replacement in time for the March 2020 presidential primary.

Georgia's voting system needed more updates than just machines. Our staff worked with Rep. Barry Fleming, who had chaired the SAFE Commission and was chairman of the House Judiciary Committee, to draft legislation, which became House Bill 316, that would, among other things:

- replace the current DRE voting machines with ballot-marking devices
- allow Georgia to join the Electronic Registration Information Center (ERIC), a multistate organization to share voter information with other states to allow for more accurate voter registration lists
- prevent changes in voting locations less than sixty days before a general primary or election
- extend the time before voters are declared inactive from three years to five years, and remove voters from rolls after eight or nine years of inactivity, only after mailing a final notification to the address on record
- conduct an audit immediately following each election to confirm election equipment worked properly
- allow legal voters with proper identification to "cure," or fix, a problem with a signature on an absentee ballot

While Fleming worked to move the legislation through Governmental Affairs Committee hearings and onto the House floor, Gabe Sterling, chief operating officer for the secretary of state, led staff members through meetings to draft the RFP. They began meeting every other day, and Gabe quickly realized they weren't moving fast enough. We wanted to put out the RFP as soon as both the House and Senate approved the bill. They met every day, and later doubled that to two meetings every day at 9:00 a.m. and 2:00 p.m.

Not only did they work fast, they had to get every word in the RFP correct. For example, nothing in the RFP could imply favoritism toward any particular vendor. Given the time crunch, we had no time for a redo because of a bid protest.

In the meantime, Deputy Secretary of State Jordan Fuchs was organizing a multidisciplinary evaluation team to review the proposals. That group included, among others, a cybersecurity expert, an advocate for people with disabilities, election directors from large and small counties (their needs are quite different from each other), and an attorney who is an expert in election law.

HB 316 cleared the General Assembly on March 14, 2019, and we immediately publicized the RFP.

Four companies submitted bids, although one missed the deadline by three hours and was disqualified.

Denver-based Dominion Voting Systems, which had the lowest bid, submitted the strongest proposal overall. At $107 million, the contract that was signed following the bid process was $43 million less than the General Assembly limit.

State law required us to provide one machine for every 250 active voters in each precinct, but that was a minimum. Our goal was that no county would have fewer new machines than they had previously.

Dominion maintained a warehouse in Smyrna, north of Atlanta, where they tested each machine and determined it was ready for state acceptance. Then we had state contractors run acceptance testing on each machine to confirm they were ready for use. After that confirmation, the machines were sealed and boxed for shipment to counties.

We shipped machines to counties from October 2019 through February 14, 2020, then we followed that with a smaller supplemental round of shipments. The total shipped gave counties one machine for about every 212 voters.

Counties maintained machines sealed in their secure warehouses until shortly before Election Day, when they delivered them to their voting locations.

CHAPTER 7
2020

GEORGIA'S PRESIDENTIAL PREFERENCE primary was scheduled for March 24, 2020. But implementing a new voting system to be ready for early voting to begin in early March was not the only challenge we faced. We also knew that we would face continued lawsuits from activist groups seeking to change Georgia law to suit their own political purposes. Given my experience dealing with all the litigation surrounding the 2018 election and successfully defending our state laws in those cases, I was ready for the fight.

FOUR PILLARS

Brian Kemp isn't the only one to defeat Stacey Abrams—we successfully defeated her effort and her allies in court as they tried to change election laws. In my time in public life, I have consistently seen Democrats attack efforts to ensure integrity in the election and voter registration processes. From photo ID laws to keeping clean voter rolls to citizenship verification, Democrats opposed every single one with inflammatory rhetoric and lawsuits. I knew the 2020 election would be no different. Given the cold-shoulder reception that national conservative groups gave us in Washington, D.C., when we told them that Georgia's election laws were certainly going to be attacked leading up to the 2020 election, I knew there would be no conservative cavalry riding in to help us match the resources of the liberal litigation machine. But I also knew that we had right on our side. Despite the characterization from Stacey Abrams and other liberal activist groups, our election laws in Georgia stood up favorably to any other state. With our outside counsel at the attorney general's office, who brought in Georgia's leading conservative election lawyers, I was confident we could successfully defend all of our election integrity measures.

In 2020, the election integrity safeguards Democrats and their allies were going to attack all seemed to surround the absentee ballot process. Due to protections like precinct-based voting, photo ID, and restrictions on campaigning and pressuring voters around polling places, in-person voting is very secure. Absentee voting is harder to secure because election officials have to verify they are dealing with the correct voter without ever seeing that voter in person.

In 2020, Democrats and their allies sought to prevent county election officials from rejecting ballots based off signature mismatches, to allow ballot harvesting (when political operatives can pick up and return a voter's absentee ballot), to extend Election Day by allowing ballots that are returned (or even voted) after Election Day to be counted, and to require local governments to foot the bill for return postage for voters who wish to vote absentee.

Marc E. Elias, an attorney who has represented numerous Democratic organizations and campaigns in election cases, called these desires his "four pillars to safeguard vote by mail," but if you read what Democratic groups actually ask for in lawsuits versus how they describe their "four pillars" in press releases, it becomes clear that, rather than attempting to safeguard voting, they are attempting to tear down common sense election integrity measures and tie the hands of local election officials.

Requiring that ballots be received no later than Election Day has been a long-standing election integrity measure in almost every state. Exceptions are states like Alaska, which, given its size, rural nature, and weather in November, has a legitimate reason to allow for late-arriving ballots that are postmarked by Election Day. If you actually read the lawsuits seeking to count late-arriving ballots, they ask courts to order that the U.S. Constitution requires that not only late-arriving ballots postmarked by Election Day be counted, but that any ballots received up to ten days after the election even without postmarks be counted unless the county election official can definitively prove that the ballot was cast after Election Day. How could a county election official ever prove that? They couldn't. So why would Democrats and their allies seek to remove this common sense election integrity measure?

Ballot harvesting is well-documented to lead to fraud. A congressional election in North Carolina was overturned in 2018 after a ballot-harvesting ring was uncovered. A political operative was found to be collecting absentee ballots from voters, not returning some of those ballots, and even voting or voiding some of those ballots with overvotes. It doesn't take a genius to know that putting a political operative between a voter and their local election officials is rife with potential for abuse. Voting should be private, and voters should be able to make their selections without pressure or interference. That Democrats saw putting political operatives between voters and their ballots being counted as something that the U.S. Constitution requires is laughable on its face. It's not a "safeguard." One of the first things I did as secretary of state was get a law passed that made it crystal clear that ballot harvesting was illegal in Georgia, and I was ready to fight to uphold that law.

Like many states, local election officials in Georgia verified an absentee voter's identity by matching the signature on the absentee ballot application and the absentee ballot with other signatures from the voter that the local election office had on file. If the signatures matched, the ballot was accepted. If they didn't, the voter received a notification that their signature did not match, and they had to submit a sworn affidavit and a copy of their ID to prove who they were prior to their ballot being counted. In my opinion, signature matching is not the best way to verify a voter's identity. It's subjective and time-intensive for local election officials, who are not signature-matching experts by any means. I have always supported moving to a photo-ID-based verification process like the one Georgia put in place following the 2020 election, but in 2020 signature matching was what the law required, and I was going to make sure that it remained in place.

As expected, liberal groups filed lawsuits seeking to usurp Georgia election law with their own policy preferences (the aforementioned "four pillars"). The first one they filed dealt with our signature-matching requirement. The Georgia Democratic Party, represented by Mark Elias, sought to "preliminarily and permanently enjoin the secretary and the state election board from enforcing parts of O.C.G.A. §21-2-386(a)(1)(C) that require election officials to reject absentee ballots based on a signature mismatch."[35] In other words, they wanted to disallow rejecting ballots when county election officials determined the signatures didn't match. That wouldn't protect voters. I knew I had to ensure that county election officials were still required to conduct signature matching and reject ballots when the signature didn't match and the issue was not cured by the voter. After the office of the Georgia attorney general and outside counsel Vincent R. Russo filed motions to dismiss the Democrats' lawsuit, the Democrats' attorneys approached our attorneys about settling the case. We felt good about our case, and the only way we would settle anything is if the Democrats admitted that signature matching would still be required for the 2020 election cycle. I think the Democrats recognized the strength of our position as well, because they agreed that signature matching would still be a requirement for the 2020 election, that uncured ballots would be rejected if county election officials determined signatures didn't match, and they would give up all their claims against Georgia's signature-matching process. Given the cost to taxpayers of continuing to litigate cases and the admission by the Democrats that signature matching would still be a requirement prior to counting any ballots, the attorney general's office recommended that we accept the settlement.

As part of the settlement, my office agreed to issue an "Official Election Bulletin" to remind county elections officials to follow procedures outlined in Georgia law regarding signature matching. Much has been made of the part of the Official Election Bulletin that recommended counties utilize an additional set of eyes prior to rejecting a ballot, but this was already common practice in Georgia. It wasn't new and it wasn't a requirement. It was a recommendation from our office on how counties could best conduct signature matching. Signature matching at both the absentee ballot application phase and when the absentee ballots were returned to the counties remained in full force. This settlement agreement was called later the "consent decree," and I was said to have signed it. Neither statement is correct.

Lawsuits addressing the other three "pillars" worked their way through the courts. Democrats sought to extend Election Day by allowing for the late return of absentee ballots, allowing political operatives to gather ballots, and placing an unfunded mandate on counties to pay voters' return postage. None of these was allowed by Georgia law. Fighting Democrats' politically motivated lawsuits was an expected challenge in the lead-up to the

2020 election, but another challenge to election administration was looming.

COVID-19

On March 12, Governor Kemp announced Georgia's first COVID-19-related death, a sixty-seven-year-old man who had tested positive three days earlier. Case numbers were increasing daily, and schools and colleges across the state announced they were shutting down. The men's NCAA basketball Final Four, the culmination of March Madness, to have been played in Atlanta, was cancelled, and the General Assembly suspended its ongoing session. The NBA season was also suspended when a player tested positive.

We were two weeks into early voting for the presidential primary, and we had a decision to make. The nominees were a forgone conclusion. President Trump had no opposition, and Joe Biden, after winning in South Carolina, was a lock for the Democratic nomination. But you can't assume winners without completing the process.

Because we had a statewide general primary scheduled for two months later, May 19, we decided to temporarily suspend all in-person voting and schedule the presidential primary for the same day.

The senior advisors for House Speaker David Ralston and my advisors conferred on the matter, and he agreed with the change. "This will ensure an orderly and safe elections process," he told the media, "and is in the best interest of Georgia's citizens."[36] The speaker was particularly concerned about the well-being of voters and poll workers and would later ask us to postpone the primary even further.

The Democratic Party of Georgia also agreed with the change. "Our priority is to protect the health and safety of all Georgians and to ensure that as many Georgians as possible have an opportunity to vote," said state Senator Nikema Williams, chairwoman of the party. "Continued in-person voting could compromise both goals."[37]

The speaker and I, however, would not agree on my next decision to protect voters from the growing threat. With social distancing as the most important tool for limiting the spread of the coronavirus, a declared state of emergency and stay-at-home sheltering, we needed to make Georgians aware of alternatives to voting in person. We decided to mail absentee ballot request forms to every active registered voter in Georgia—not live absentee ballots but absentee ballot request forms. No-excuse absentee voting has been in law since 2005, voted and pushed by Republicans.

Ryan Germany, the general counsel in our office, reached out to the governor's office and explained our plan, and Jordan Fuchs, deputy secretary of state, called the office of the lieutenant governor and the speaker of the house and explained to each of them what we were doing.

We had to work quickly, even with the postponed primary date. I made the announcement on March 24, and we had the requests and envelopes printed and ready to go in a record time of six days.

Speaker Ralston disagreed, suggesting another delay in the primary would address the safety concerns without the need to mail absentee ballot request forms. In a letter to me on March 26, he wrote, "Pushing the primary back a month or more gives us more time to allow the situation to improve so that voters can vote in the manner in which they are most familiar."

I agreed in theory with him that the ideal system is for everybody to show up and vote on Tuesday. Of course, it would not be easy cramming 2 million Georgians through the voting booths in one day, so realistically, we do need early voting. And there is an appropriate place for absentee voting because people travel, they get sick, and they have situations that prevent them from getting to the polls on Election Day. But I believe in-person voting with a photo ID, so there's no question who's voting, is the best possible system.

The speaker recommended scheduling the primary for June 23 or later, and Georgia law allowed me to postpone an election for forty-five days during a state of emergency. But the governor's order was scheduled to expire on April 13, more than a month before the rescheduled primary. Unless the governor extended the state of emergency, I could not delay the primary again.

On Monday, March 30, we began mailing 6.9 million absentee ballot request forms to active, registered voters. That process also started the clock on anyone whose mail bounced back. For example, if the post office reported that a voter no longer lived at that particular address, the voter's name was moved to "inactive" status, a required step before removing a voter from the voter rolls. Mailing out absentee ballot applications in May allowed us to flag individuals who no longer lived in the state and also prevented liberal judges from forcing the state to mail ballots—not just applications—for the November election.

By coincidence, that same morning President Trump appeared on *Fox & Friends* and said he opposed the idea of expanded voting by mail. It was a theme he repeated throughout the campaign—a theme that may have cost him a second term.

Three days after Trump made his opposition to voting by mail clear, and while the ballot request forms were moving through the mail to voters, Speaker Ralston announced his own objections. "This will be extremely devastating to Republicans and conservatives in Georgia," he told the media. "Every registered voter will get one of these. . . . This will certainly drive up turnout."[38]

I also made my position clear:

Times of turbulence and upheaval like the one we Georgians face require decisive action if the liberties we hold so dear are to be preserved. I am acting today because the people of Georgia, from the earliest settlers to heroes like Rev. Dr. Martin Luther King Jr., have fought too long and too hard for their right to vote to have it curtailed. Georgia has faced challenges before and overcome them, and we can do so again through the grit and ingenuity that has made America a shining example for democracies around the world.[39]

Georgia began offering no-excuse absentee voting in 2005, supported by both David Ralston and Sen. David Shafer (currently Georgia Republican Party Chairman) and signed by Republican Governor Sonny Perdue. The law allowed voters, for any reason, to request an absentee ballot. In the intervening years, 5 to 6 percent of Georgia voters utilized absentee ballots.

We knew we were going to have a significant increase in absentee voting in 2020 because of the pandemic. We also believed if we didn't send out ballot requests, political organizations and some county election boards would distribute requests for ballots while others would not. So if Fulton, DeKalb, Clayton, and Chatham counties sent ballot applications to all of their voters and Cherokee and Forsyth counties did not, then thousands more Democratic than Republican voters would request ballots. Replicate that in all of the large metropolitan counties, and there's a huge disparity in access to the polls. By sending out absentee ballot applications, we leveled the playing field, making sure all Georgians were aware of the laws and had access to absentee ballots.

Additionally, candidates and other political groups would send out ballot requests until voters had a stack of five or six of them. Some of those voters might send in multiple applications, further burdening county elections offices—when their workers were at home because the county offices were closed!

The best way to manage the situation was a uniform process to ensure a smooth rollout.

My team made phone calls and sent texts to inform the governor, lieutenant governor, speaker of the house, and Republican and Democratic state party officials that we were going to mail out absentee ballot request forms to active, registered voters. We were under a huge time crunch, and I knew that doing nothing for Georgia's voters was not an option in the middle of the pandemic.

Our office would continue to put the voters above the politically driven demands of either party.

Voters were instructed to return the absentee ballot requests to their county elections offices, where election officials confirmed the signature on the form matched the signature they had on file. The counties then input the voter information and issued the voter an absentee ballot.

An additional benefit of sending out the ballot request forms was that the post office returned about 300,000 of our envelopes to our office as undeliverable, so we knew those people had moved. Due to federal law constraints (National Voters Registration Act of 1993), we couldn't remove the voters immediately, but the law did allow us to put them on an inactive list, identifying them for later removal. Frustratingly, when the Republicans controlled the U.S. House, Senate, and presidency from 2017 to 2019, no legislation by Republicans was proposed on reforming NVRA.

Congressman Hice, my opponent for the 2022 Republican primary, never authored or proposed any election reform legislation during his three terms in Congress, yet, amazingly, election reform is his new hot-button issue.

We contracted with Runbeck Election Services to print the absentee ballots and mail them to voters after the ballot applications were received and the counties matched signatures. This took the pressure off the counties, which were working at limited capacity.

Almost all of Georgia's 159 counties managed to confirm absentee ballot requests and forward information to our office smoothly. A few did not. Fulton County, Georgia's largest, was overwhelmed by more than 140,000 absentee ballot requests. They fell behind and never caught up.

In late March, Fulton County's registration chief came down with COVID-19, then an elections employee there, Beverly Walker, passed away of coronavirus on April 15. The county's elections office was closed for two days for cleaning and decontamination, but Beverly Walker's death meant much more than that. She had been a long-time employee and was described in local media as a maternal figure in the office.

ANOTHER EXTENSION

On April 8, Governor Kemp extended the state of emergency until May 13. Although the extension did not include the actual primary day, it did cover almost every day of in-person voting, and I felt comfortable exercising the power vested in me by Georgia law to postpone the primary election until June 9.

Speaker Ralston, still upset over our decision to mail ballot requests, told the media, "Having arrived at this inevitable conclusion after unnecessarily spending millions of additional taxpayer dollars, we can now move forward on a more realistic timeline that inspires confidence on the part of poll workers and voters alike."[40]

Rescheduling the primary was not inevitable. I had no legal authority to make the change until the governor extended the state of emergency. When he did, I acted within twenty-four hours to protect the health and safety of Georgia voters and poll workers.

Democrats hurled complaints as well. "Delaying Georgia's election does not ensure either public safety or Georgians' right to vote," Saira Draper of the Democratic Party of Georgia told *The Atlanta Journal-Constitution*. She defined "safety" and the "right to vote" as "providing paid postage, counting all ballots postmarked by election day, and mailing vote-by-mail ballots to all registered voters, not just some."[41] She had listed three of the Democrat's Four Pillars, but none was allowed by Georgia law.

Throughout the crisis, our office remained in close contact with county election officials across the state. In early April, reports of mounting difficulties from county election officials, particularly in southwest Georgia, grew to a point where these officials could not overcome the challenges brought on by COVID-19 in time for in-person voting to begin on April 27.

Modeling by the Centers for Disease Control and Prevention and by the Institute for Health Metrics and Evaluation projected the COVID-19 pandemic in Georgia would peak around April 24, only days before in-person voting was scheduled to begin.

We knew challenges would remain on June 9, but we believed the additional three weeks would give our office and counties time to shore up contingency plans, find and train additional poll workers, and procure supplies and equipment necessary to clean equipment and protect poll workers.

Sometimes elections happen in less-than-ideal circumstances. Speaker Ralston had asked that we push the primary to June 23, and I thoughtfully considered his concerns, but further delay could have had negative consequences on our preparation for the November 3 general election. Given the existing deadlines to prepare and send ballots for the November election, particularly for military and overseas voters, moving forward on June 9 was the best way to ensure a successful election year in Georgia.

◆ ◆ ◆

After two delays, we were still concerned about the counties' ability to staff polling places across the state. Georgia historically has relied on its older, retired citizens to work long hours at the polls on Election Day. Because of the pandemic, many of those workers decided the risk to their health was too great.

We made sure counties were familiar with CDC guidelines to keep voters and workers safe with Plexiglas dividers, plenty of disinfectant wipes, face shields, and a plan for using them.

Gabe Sterling, our chief operating officer, checked in on the counties, especially the large counties, regularly.

"Are you going to have enough people to work the polls?" he asked.

"Yes, we're good," they said.

"Are you sure?"

"We're sure."

"Absolutely sure?"

"Absolutely."

We were also concerned about training. The pandemic prevented in-person training, so most poll workers would be touching the new machines for the first time on Election Day. The state and counties created online training materials for poll workers, and we followed up with communications to county officials to make sure everybody felt confident in their understanding. There were the typical jitters one would expect when using a new system for the first time, but overall, our county election officials were confident and prepared.

We were still trying to protect voters and election officials from exposure to COVID-19 by emphasizing absentee voting. At the same time, President Trump continued attacking this process that more and more states were utilizing to protect their citizens. On May 26, a week before the Georgia primary, Trump wrote on Twitter and Facebook, "There is NO WAY (ZERO!) that Mail-In Ballots will be anything less than substantially fraudulent. Mail boxes will be robbed, ballots will be forged & even illegally printed out & fraudulently signed."[42]

Counties were also losing voting places by the dozens because of the pandemic. Schools, churches, and senior centers across the state became unavailable. Where counties were unable to identify alternative sites, they consolidated voting locations. In Atlanta, for example, voters from two precincts would be voting at the Lutheran Church of the Redeemer on Peachtree Street. When the church said they could not serve as a voting site during the pandemic, those precincts were combined with three others at Grady High School, about a mile away. However, the school was closed, so the county reached out to Park Tavern, a restaurant and event space in Piedmont Park, across the street from Grady High School.

The combined five precincts voting at Park Tavern had more than 16,000 active registered voters. We continued to encourage voters to use the absentee ballots they had requested, returning them by mail or using the secure drop boxes many counties had made available. Still, we anticipated longer-than-usual lines on Tuesday.

Many Fulton County voters, it turned out, had not received their absentee ballots a week before the primary. Fearful of being disenfranchised, they drove to the eight early voting sites around the county and waited in line for hours to vote—a sign of things to come.

Then, on the Friday night before the June primary, Fulton County put out the word that they needed 250 poll workers. Gabe was beside himself. There was no way to properly train 250 people over the weekend or on Monday to be ready on Tuesday morning. As it turned out, hundreds of poll workers saw the new voting machines for the first time on Tuesday morning, having received all of their training online.

By 7:00 a.m. on Tuesday morning, anybody driving past the Park Tavern voting site could predict it was going to be an all-day logistical nightmare. More than 350 socially distanced voters were already standing in line when the doors opened. Park Tavern turned out to be one of the top producing locations in the state, processing 160 voters an hour. But even at that rate, the waiting time to vote was already more than two hours long. They wouldn't catch up until late that night.

The problem wasn't too few voting machines. The hang-up almost always happens with voter check-in and at the ballot scanners on the back end. The Wednesday morning all-caps headline on the front page of *The Atlanta Journal-Constitution* screamed, "COMPLETE MELTDOWN."[43]

Once again we heard cries of "voter suppression!" Somehow, the media said, the Republican secretary of state's office had created the meltdown in Fulton and DeKalb counties. I first explained that "counties run elections," we have 159 counties, and more than 150 of them did a great job. Unfortunately, the county that struggles most happens to be the largest in the middle of the South's largest media market. People see lines in Fulton County and assume we have lines in every county in the state. Or they assume that because Fulton is predominately Democratic, that Republican state leadership connived to suppress voting there.

But the county officials and election boards select the voting locations, train poll workers, distribute voting machines, and manage almost every Election Day decision.

The flip side of that argument, also false, was that predominantly Democratic counties were in on some sort of fix. Counties struggle sometimes because, frankly, a few of them are in over their heads. Large counties require well-run, complex organizations to set up hundreds of voting sites for hundreds of thousands of voters.

I often call out Fulton County, whose mismanagement issues are documented dating back to the early 1990s, because of their refusal to address the logistical issues they seem to have every election cycle. It is commonly understood that if something is going to go wrong during an election in Georgia, it's going to happen in Fulton County. Their mismanagement breeds distrust and conspiracy theories. Want to know the real reason why Fulton has long lines? It's not because Republicans are suppressing them. It's because they do not adequately staff their polling locations or train their poll workers. This issue is in the complete control of Fulton County's Democratic leadership.

Days after the primary, Gabe Sterling went to work with line-management software developed by the Massachusetts Institute of Technology. He analyzed all 2,600 voting locations in the state and gave the data to counties making decisions where to allocate machines and personnel. He set the program for a twenty-minute wait time and used a color-coded grid to show how much equipment and how many poll workers would be required to meet that goal.

Also in the wake of the primary election problems, the state election board investigated issues around the primary in Fulton County. We can't tolerate management issues when they affect citizens' ability to cast a vote. The franchise is too precious.

Our office received 254 complaints from voters who did not receive an absentee ballot, and at least 107 of those people did not vote at all in the June 9 primary. At least 105 were never entered into the eNet voter registration system, meaning the county never entered the voters' information for ballot fulfillment. Testimony also revealed many more voters didn't receive a requested absentee ballot, evidenced in the large numbers that went to the poll and reported not receiving a ballot.

Democratic appointee David Worley made a motion to send the case to the Georgia attorney general, saying, "While the COVID phenomenon . . . was not limited to Fulton . . . the large extent of problems with the processing of absentee ballot applications were clearly evident in Fulton County, and now that the case is before us, I don't think we can ignore that. And if one person being denied their right to vote is too many, 250 is certainly too many."[44]

All of us on the state level and those doing the hard work at the county level had to manage through the COVID-19 crisis in June, and we would have to manage through it in November as well. But the volume of Fulton's issues was unique—up to 80 percent of the complaints we received in Georgia were concerning Fulton County.

Our investigation led to a consent order between the county and the State Election Board requiring Fulton to engage an independent elections expert to monitor the general election process. The monitor, Carter Jones, would spend more than 250 hours onsite observing the county's preparation and execution of the November general election and the January runoff. This is the first time I know of that a secretary of state has finally held Fulton County accountable for its mismanagement and disorganization in a manner that required actual change, not just lip service.

Soon after the November election, Carter Jones prepared a formal report that was widely disseminated by the press, and he shared his findings and observations in separate briefings with secretary of state staff and myself, the State Election Board, Fulton County Election Board, and the Fulton County Commissioners. I again called for the termination of the Fulton County election director. The Fulton County Election Board, which consists of three Democrats and two Republicans, voted 3-2 to terminate the election director. The Democrat who joined the Republicans in this vote was not renominated by the Democratic Party. The Fulton County Commission, which consists of four Democrats and three Republicans, voted to reinstate the election director in a 4-3 vote. Recently passed legislation by the General Assembly in 2021 in Senate Bill 202 provides an accountability procedure for replacing failing county election management.

◆ ◆ ◆

As we prepared for an anticipated record-breaking general election, we continued to litigate and successfully combat the Democratic Party's Four Pillars. When it came to free or prepaid postage, the Democrats argued that a 55-cent stamp amounted to a poll tax and an unjustifiable burden on the right to vote. Judge Amy Totenberg in the Northern District of Georgia disagreed, writing on August 11:

"The fact that any registered voter may vote in Georgia on election day without purchasing a stamp, and without undertaking any 'extra steps' besides showing up at the voting precinct and complying with generally applicable election regulations, necessitates a conclusion that stamps are not poll taxes."[45]

Then, on August 31, Federal District Court Judge Eleanor Ross ruled that Georgia had to accept absentee ballots postmarked by Election Day and received within three days. I immediately directed our attorneys to appeal her decision—Georgia law requires ballots be received by Election Day—and a three-judge panel of the Eleventh Circuit Court of Appeals issued a stay of the order on October 2.

The appeals court wrote:

> Georgia's decades-old absentee ballot deadline is both reasonable and nondiscriminatory. . . . [Voters] can return their ballots through the mail, hand-delivery, or a drop box; dozens of drop boxes are available through Election Day in numerous locations, and all jurisdictions have the authority to add them. Voters also have the option to participate in early in-person voting. And though delays in the postal service may (not will) delay when some voters receive their absentee ballots, all of these avenues remain open to any and all voters. . . . The Constitution sets out our sphere of decision making, and that sphere does not extend to second-guessing and interfering with a State's reasonable, nondiscriminatory election rules. COVID-19 has not put any gloss on the Constitution's demand that States—not federal courts—are in charge of setting those rules. Because Georgia's decades-old Election Day deadline for absentee ballots does not threaten voting and is justified by a host of interests, we stay the district court's injunction of that deadline.[46]

Traditionally, no-excuse absentee ballots had been a Republican strength in Georgia, not a weakness, and they could have remained so in 2020. Republicans established no-excuse absentee ballots because their voters were more likely to use them. Then utilization exploded in 2020 because of COVID-19.

In the months between the primary and the general elections, we developed a web page for absentee ballot request forms and implemented a photo ID requirement for making those requests—I was the first Georgia secretary of state to have absentee ballots associated with photo ID. The online portal was fast, efficient, and secure.

Joe Biden made the best of the situation and embraced the absentee ballots; Donald Trump ridiculed them. Both candidates voted absentee. Let that sink in.

Then consider the math: 46 percent of voters nationwide utilized absentee ballots. Historically, that would have worked out great for Republican candidates in Georgia. But Trump's drumbeat against absentee voting continued all the way through the November general election, and it was a terrible disservice to himself and other Republicans.

Republicans typically listen to their leadership, and their leader was telling them not to vote absentee. That was a risky strategy for several reasons. First, most Georgia Republicans expected Donald Trump to win our state. With about 2,000 new COVID-19 cases every day in Georgia, voters planning to vote in person on Election Day might lose that opportunity if they contracted the virus or were exposed to it and had to be quarantined.

For weeks leading up to the election, the Democratic Party was pushing absentee ballots and early voting. After years of Republican dominance, Democrats had figured out how to drive absentee ballots. In the 2018 gubernatorial election, Stacey Abrams received 53,709 more absentee votes than Brian Kemp. They turned that switch up about five notches in 2020. They called and texted registered Democrats again and again: "I noticed you haven't gotten your absentee ballot back. Are you going to send it back in?" Or they would tell voters where they could vote early. Friends told me their children were getting these messages constantly. Those conversations clarified two things: the Democratic Party had a strong ground game for driving absentee votes, and my friends' children were part of their target demographic.

On the Republican side, we just didn't see that kind of grassroots effort. Republicans were flying at 60,000 feet, relying on a top-down approach. It was all about President Trump generating votes with rallies and tweets.

On the Sunday night before Election Day, President Trump held a rally in Rome, Georgia. After two decades as a Republican stronghold, Georgia had officially transformed into a battleground state, and thirty-six hours before the polls opened, Trump was battling.

Four million Georgians had already voted early or by absentee ballot—almost as many as the state's total record voter turnout. Still, we expected up to 2 million more people to vote in person on Tuesday. Trump's chances in Georgia depended on a big Election Day. Voters had made up their minds. To win, Trump needed to get his voters to the polls.

CHAPTER 8
SIXTY DAYS OF DISINFORMATION

JUST UNDER A MILLION GEORGIA VOTERS CAME to the polls on Election Day—nearly 174,000 more than in the June primary— and the average wait time statewide was less than two minutes. A few precincts reported thirty- and forty-minute waits during the busiest parts of the day. County officials had ironed out the problems they experienced in June and ran their operations smoothly.

But turnout was several hundred thousand fewer than anticipated, and that did not bode well for President Trump. For months he had insisted that mail-in, or absentee, ballots were "fraudulent," and many Georgia Republicans listened. They had not sent absentee ballots, so we expected them to show up on Election Day. Many of them did not.

It did not take long for the president to start blaming everybody but himself for falling short. Among those he blamed were election officials.

Thinking of the thousands of election officials, from secretaries of state to poll workers who checked in millions of voters across the country on Election Day, I was reminded of Psalm 1:

That person is like a tree planted by streams of water,

which yields its fruit in season

and whose leaf does not wither—

> *whatever they do prospers.*
>
> — Psalm 1:3, NIV

Poll workers—your neighbors, many of them older—knew they were risking COVID-19 in the middle of the pandemic. Some became infected. But they accepted the risk to ensure a free and fair election. They did not expect verbal attacks and threats from Trump and his supporters.

We had to stand strong. I thought of my father, who quietly went about his business and told the truth, and I drew strength from him. My job was to stand in the gap and take the abuse. President Trump made me the most visible of his targets, but I was not alone. The professionals in the secretary of state's office and other election officials around the country defended the truth.

Earlier in the book I tried to answer the question that many have asked. Where did you get the strength or fortitude to stand up and not buckle? How did you hold your composure and not lash back? As I wrote this book, it gave me cause for reflection. And I remember when my dad gave one of my sons a cloth scroll that his father had given him. My son hung it on his wall and took it with him to college. On it was the poem by Rudyard Kipling titled "If":

If you can keep your head when all about you

Are losing theirs and blaming it on you,

If you can trust yourself when all men doubt you,

But make allowance for their doubting too;

If you can wait and not be tired by waiting,

Or being lied about, don't deal in lies,

Or being hated, don't give way to hating,

And yet don't look too good, nor talk too wise:

If you can dream—and not make dreams your master;

If you can think—and not make thoughts your aim;

If you can meet with Triumph and Disaster

And treat those two impostors just the same;

If you can bear to hear the truth you've spoken

Twisted by knaves to make a trap for fools,

Or watch the things you gave your life to, broken,

And stoop and build 'em up with worn-out tools:

If you can make one heap of all your winnings

And risk it on one turn of pitch-and-toss,

And lose, and start again at your beginnings

And never breathe a word about your loss;

If you can force your heart and nerve and sinew

To serve your turn long after they are gone,

And so hold on when there is nothing in you

Except the Will which says to them: "Hold on!"

If you can talk with crowds and keep your virtue,

Or walk with Kings—nor lose the common touch,

If neither foes nor loving friends can hurt you,

If all men count with you, but none too much;

If you can fill the unforgiving minute

With sixty seconds' worth of distance run,

Yours is the Earth and everything that's in it,

And—which is more—you'll be a Man, my son![47]

I strive to keep my wits about me, to be respectful of everyone's positional authority, particularly our nation's highest officeholder, and to be true to what matters most in this job: the Constitution and laws of our state and nation.

For sixty days, from Election Day until January 2, when President Trump called and asked me to "find 11,780 votes," we investigated all complaints received and looked for any evidence of widespread fraud. There is no such thing as a perfect election. Whenever millions of people have to go to the right place at the right time and the workers at those polling locations have to properly perform their duties, issues will come up. We saw the same types of issues following the 2020 election that have occurred after all recent elections in Georgia—voters going to the wrong location (sometimes directly encouraged to do so by political interest groups), poll workers forgetting the keys to the building leading to a polling place and opening up late, and minor equipment issues that are easily solved if poll workers are properly trained. We did not see any evidence of widespread fraud.

Even President Trump's own Department of Justice appointee found zero evidence to back up the president's claims. When U.S. Attorney Byung J. "BJay" Pak resigned as head of the Atlanta office of the United States Justice Department, President Trump appointed U. S. Attorney Bobby Christine from Augusta as acting head of the Atlanta office. Mr. Christine had been a member of our Absentee Ballot Fraud Task Force from its inception.

A January 12, 2021, article in *The Atlanta Journal-Constitution* reported, "The acting U.S. attorney for Northern Georgia, who was named after his predecessor reportedly angered President Trump for not finding election fraud, told staffers in a conference call Monday that he dismissed two election fraud cases on his first day."[48]

"I would love to stand out on the street corner and scream this, and I can't," said Bobby Christine, according to an audio recording of the call obtained by the *AJC*. "But I can tell you I closed the two most—I don't know, I guess you'd call them high profile or the two most pressing election issues this office has. I said I believe, as many of the people around the table believed, there's just nothing to them."[49]

On the same day, *The Washington Post* reported Mr. Christine telling his staff, "We don't have these huge colossal issues that if you turn on the TV, you'd think it'd be," he said.[50]

One of the main reasons I wrote this book was to create a historical record of the sixty days between Election Day 2020 and President Trump's widely discussed January 2, 2021, telephone call to me. So here, for the rest of the book, I will do two things: First, I will give a day-by-day breakdown of what was happening, and second, I will walk you through that phone call point-by-point, quoting the president, his chief of staff, myself, my staff, and all the lawyers on both sides. In addition, I will add my observations, providing the full, detailed answers the president didn't want to hear.

NOVEMBER 4

"THIS IS GETTING REALLY UGLY"

When I left the house for the capitol on Wednesday morning, Tricia was packing for a trip to the Great Smoky Mountains. She was co-leading a group of wildlife photographers on a weekend field trip—an annual event for the group—and she went up a day early to prep. She didn't give another thought to the election after she got up there, and I was glad of that.

When she's holding a camera, she says, "It's the only time in life where I completely live in the moment. I forget about time, I forget about eating, I forget about everything. I'm just in the moment with whatever I'm trying to capture, and it's so fulfilling. I've always marveled at God's creation and have finally found a way to capture just the tiniest snapshot of His glory through my photography."

The truth and beauty of Tricia's photography astounds me, whether it's photos of our grandchildren, landscapes, or the flowers in our backyard. In every photo she takes, it's like a little bit of herself is added into it. I can always tell when it is her work, because it reveals a little bit of how she sees the world around her.

I was hoping to see her up there on Friday after the counties had finished counting votes. In the meantime, I spent Wednesday morning at the capitol giving interviews with the network and cable television news shows updating the public on the progress of tallying results. Every show announced on its screen something like:

Breaking News: All Eyes on Georgia.
Secretary of State on Ballot Count and What's Next

President Trump was leading, but several large metropolitan counties still had thousands of absentee ballots to count. We had a long way to go.

On Wednesday afternoon in Savannah, the Trump campaign and the Georgia Republican Party filed a lawsuit claiming that fifty-three absentee ballots had been received after 7:00 p.m. on Election Day and then mixed in with other ballots for counting. They asked the county to secure and account for any ballots received after 7:00 p.m. A hearing was scheduled for Thursday morning. The state of Georgia and my office were not a party to the lawsuit, but we would be watching the courtroom closely.

In the Great Smoky Mountains, Tricia wasn't keeping up with any of that. Then, as she was getting ready for bed, her phone pinged with a text at 10:06 p.m. from an unidentified caller:

Hi Patricia. This is getting really ugly. Do Brad a favor and tell him to step down immediately.

A stranger knew who she was, had gotten her cell number, and had sent her a text. She was unnerved and thought about calling me, but she decided to wait until morning. I was still hoping to drive up late Friday.

NOVEMBER 5

"THE COURT FINDS THAT THERE IS NO EVIDENCE"

After a one-hour hearing on Thursday morning, Chatham Superior Court Judge James Bass denied the Trump campaign's petition. The Trump campaign and the Georgia Republican Party told the court that a poll watcher had seen absentee ballots received after the 7:00 p.m. Election Day deadline being mixed with other ballots.

"Having read and considered said petition, all argument and evidence of record, including the evidence presented at the hearing, and the applicable law," the judge wrote, "the Court finds that there is no evidence that the ballots referenced in the petition were received after 7:00 p.m. on Election Day."[51]

That's the way all of the Trump campaign's lawsuits would go.

Courts demand evidence. People can say what they want on Twitter or even in a legislative hearing, but in a court of law, witnesses must tell the truth or risk a perjury charge, and lawyers who lie in a courtroom risk disbarment.

When the truth was presented to the judge, he dismissed the case.

Court after court would reject Trump's lawsuits in Georgia, except for the cases that the campaign withdrew itself.

In Washington, D.C., in the weeks leading up to Election Day, the Cybersecurity and Infrastructure Security Agency (CISA) augmented its commitment to protecting the 2020 election with a "Rumor Control" web page. "Mis- and disinformation can undermine public confidence in the electoral process, as well as in our democracy," the CISA page warned.[52]

CISA was created in 2018 under President Trump, who nominated Christopher Krebs to serve as its first director. The web page (cisa.gov/rumorcontrol) was "designed to debunk common misinformation and disinformation narratives and themes that relate broadly to the security of election infrastructure and related processes."[53] In early November, it also made Chris Krebs a target of President Trump.

Shortly after Election Day, CISA posted the following statement:

> *Over the last four years, the Cybersecurity and Infrastructure Security Agency (CISA) has been a part of a whole-of-nation effort to ensure American voters decide American elections. Importantly, after millions of Americans voted, we have no evidence any foreign adversary was capable of preventing Americans from voting or changing vote tallies.*[54]

NOVEMBER 6

ANTICIPATING A RECOUNT

Gabe Sterling and I held a press conference at the capitol on Friday morning. We had fewer than 5,500 votes left to be counted from four counties, and we were still waiting for the final military ballots to arrive by the close of business. Georgia was still too close to call. It was clear that I was going nowhere that weekend. I told the media:

> *The focus for our office and for the county election officials for now remains on making sure that every legal vote is counted and*

recorded accurately. As we are closing in on a final count, we can begin to look toward our next steps. With a margin that small, there will be a recount in Georgia. Interest in our election obviously goes far beyond Georgia's borders. The final tally in Georgia at this point has huge implications for the entire country.

The stakes are high and emotions are high on all sides. We will not let those debates distract us from our work. We will get it right, and we'll defend the integrity of our elections.

In some states, there are complaints about monitors not being allowed to watch the count. In Georgia, this process is and will remain open and transparent to monitors. If any member of the public raises legitimate concerns, we'll investigate those.

We are committed to doing anything and everything to maintaining trust in our elections process for every Georgian, regardless of partisan preference.[55]

Then Gabe addressed the media: "We are not seeing widespread irregularities. We're not seeing anything widespread. We are investigating any credible accusation with any real evidence behind it. But let me tell you one thing, when you have a narrow margin, little, small things can make a difference. So everything's going to have to be investigated to protect the integrity of the vote."[56]

Gabe grew up in Georgia, but he talks very fast. No reporter can keep up with him with a pen; they have to record him, and listen later at a slower speed, especially when he talks about technical issues.

A reporter asked him, "What is the physical recount? What would that look like? Is that scanning all the ballots through the machines again?"

"You're going to let me get into my fun geek time now to go over the SEB rules that we outlined when we passed this law," Gabe replied smiling. He added:

This is the way it's going to work. As I mentioned to y'all yesterday, the secretary directed that we procure in the original procurement, the high-speed ICCs, which are the high-capacity, high-speed scanners. They will be used at the central offices for this recount.

Now, how we're going to do that is we're going to take a deck of ballots. We are going to have those hand-counted going by what is written on the human readable portion of that. We'll tally those and we'll get a count and write it down. We will then run those through the scanners and they ought to match.

And once we validate that that scanner is scanning properly, we will then be scanning every single ballot again on the central scanners.[57]

Gabe told the reporters he thought the initial count would be completed on Friday night, assuming the mail didn't deliver thousands of additional military and overseas ballots.

And, of course, there were more questions about investigations.

"If somebody has a credible complaint," he said, "and they have some kind of evidence or some kind of trail to an evidence, they can give our office a call. And if they're in another state, give your state office a call because we want to make sure we protect the integrity of the ballot, because that's the way you're going to build faith back into the system that the outcome of the election is correct."[58]

NOVEMBER 8

LOOKING FOR SCAPEGOATS

The Trump campaign announced that Rep. Doug Collins, who finished third behind Raphael Warnock and Kelly Loeffler in the race for U.S. Senate, would lead an effort to find "irregularities that will prove that President Trump won Georgia."[59]

When you lose an election, I imagine it hurts your ego, be it a run for a county commission seat or a run for president. You believe in your heart that you did a good job, and if you never lack self-doubt, it must be doubly debilitating—and confusing. Instead of accepting a defeat, you look for scapegoats, shift blame, or seek alternative theories.

Sadly, President Trump's most trusted advisers and long-standing friends fed him a string of disinformation and misinformation—junk theories and allegations our office quickly debunked almost daily.

NOVEMBER 9

A STATEMENT THAT SAYS MORE ABOUT THEM THAN ME

Monday afternoon, six days after Election Day, Georgia's two United States senators put their political futures in the hands of President Trump. David Perdue and Kelly Loeffler wrote a joint statement calling for my resignation.

They offered no examples of failures in their statement or to the media when asked for particulars. Instead, they wrote, "There have been too many failures in Georgia elections this year and the most recent election has shined a national light on the problems.

"The mismanagement and lack of transparency from the Secretary of State is unacceptable," they continued, with no details.

"Honest elections are paramount to the foundation of our democracy," they wrote, and on that we can all agree.

But then they suggested, again without evidence, "The Secretary of State has failed to deliver honest and transparent elections. He has failed the people of Georgia, and he should step down immediately." [60]

At 3:21 p.m., seventeen minutes after the release of their statement, President Trump tweeted, "Georgia will be a big presidential win, as it was the night of the Election!" [61]

The coordination between the senators and the White House was obvious.

I met David Perdue many times and considered him to be a Republican colleague. I knew Kelly Loeffler less well, although Tricia and I had talked with her at the 2019 White House Christmas. Both senators seemed like nice people, reasonable people, the kind of people who might call if they had a problem with you.

Maybe they thought they were throwing me to the wolves. I'll never know. But I believe their statement said much more about them than it did about me and my staff.

I responded to their statement:

Earlier today Senators Loeffler and Perdue called for my resignation.

Let me start by saying that is not going to happen. The voters of Georgia hired me, and the voters will be the ones to fire me. As Secretary of State, I'll continue to fight every day to ensure fair elections in Georgia, that every legal vote counts, and that illegal votes don't count.

I know emotions are running high. Politics are involved in everything right now. If I was Senator Perdue, I'd be irritated I was in a runoff. And both Senators and I are all unhappy with the potential outcome for our President.

But I am the duly elected Secretary of State. One of my duties involves helping to run elections for all Georgia voters. I have taken that oath and I will execute that duty and follow Georgia law.[62]

NOVEMBER 10

A LAUNDRY LIST OF RUMORS

Rumors rolled in faster than we or CISA's Rumor Control could respond. In a letter to me, Doug Collins and David Shafer, representing the Trump campaign and the Georgia Republican Party respectively, elevated a laundry list of rumors by calling them "substantiated documentary, testimonial, and expert evidence" of "discrepancy and error" in the secretary of state's office.[63] But they were just rumors.

Collins and Shafer alleged ineligible out-of-state voters, deceased voters casting ballots, duplicate ballots cast by voters, and absentee ballots cast without signatures, among others.

We investigated each of these allegations that could be investigated—some claims didn't even contain enough basic facts to allow an investigation. Our investigators were not able to find any evidence supporting the claims Collins and Shafer were pushing.

They even quoted Gabe Sterling from a news conference four days earlier when he said:

> If somebody has a credible complaint and they have some kind of evidence or some kind of trail to any evidence, they can give our office a call. . . . because we want to make sure we protect the integrity of the ballot, because that's the way you're going to build faith back into the system that the outcome of the election is correct.[64]

But the evidence did not support their claims.

The same afternoon, I received a letter from Republican members and members-elect of Georgia's congressional delegation asking us to investigate the same issues raised by Collins and Shafer.

In the weeks immediately following the election, investigators in the secretary of state's office found no evidence of widespread voter fraud or any of the other issues Collins, Shafer, President Trump, and others raised.

Six months later, as I write this book, our office still has not received from Collins, Shafer, our congressional delegation, President Trump, or anyone else any kind of evidence or trail to evidence of widespread voter fraud. Just like the "voter suppression" allegations made during the 2018 election in Georgia, the claims get a lot of attention from sympathetic media when they are made. But once investigations are complete and the claims are proven false, that sympathetic media seems less interested in going back to correct the record.

NOVEMBER 11 - VETERANS DAY

"SECRETARY OF STATE STANDS UP FOR THE FACTS"

I always think of my father on Veterans Day, and I began the Wednesday press conference by talking with the media about him. Dad was seventeen years old when he graduated from high school in 1944, and he walked straight to the enlistment office in Johnstown, Pennsylvania, his hometown, to join the Marines. But when the enlistment officer realized Dad was color-blind, he rejected him.

So Dad walked down to the Navy office and somehow was able to get through the process and sign up. This was near the end of the war, of course, and the Navy was shipping everybody to the Pacific. Dad always downplayed his contribution to the war effort and, instead, remembered his friends and neighbors from Johnstown who didn't come home. A family down the street had only one son, and he was killed in action.

Tricia's dad was in the British Royal Air Force, and he was shot down over France but survived.

That generation was tremendously patriotic.

"And one of the things that they fought for," I said at the press conference, "is for our right to have free and fair elections. So that is, at the end of the day, what we do need to be mindful of, particularly in our office, as we work finishing up and closing out the election."[65]

With that in mind, I invited several county election directors from across the state, large and small counties, Republican and Democratic counties, to stand with me on the capitol steps. "They and their staff are the ones that do the hard work on the ground of making sure that all legal votes will be counted," I said. "Their job is hard. They executed their responsibilities, and they did their job."[66]

Then I announced that their jobs were about to become significantly more difficult. House Bill 316, passed in 2019, required us to conduct a risk-limiting audit (RLA) of one race from each biennial general election. The RLA requires us to select a random statistical sample of ballots from across the state and confirm that a hand tally agreed with the computer count. By law, the sample had to be large enough to be statistically significant to provide a minimum 90 percent confidence interval that the outcome was correct.

I decided to take it a step further—a big step further—with a 100 percent hand recount of all 5,026,684 ballots from the presidential election. At the end of process, we would be 100 percent certain the numbers were correct, and conclusively prove that the machines did not flip any votes, as rumors were alleging on social media. And with a November 20 deadline for certification, the counties had nine days to complete the work.

"It will be an audit, a recount, and a recanvass all at once," I said. "It will be a heavy lift, but we will work with the counties to get this done in time for our state certification. Many of these workers will be working plenty of overtime. We have all worked hard to bring fair and accurate counts to assure that the will of the voters is reflected in the final count, and that every voter will have confidence in the outcome, whether their candidate won or lost."[67]

A member of the media asked if we were conducting a hand recount because of pressure from President Trump.

"No," I said, "we're doing this because it is really what makes the most sense. With the national significance of this race and the closeness of this race, we have to run a statewide audit. This is the race that makes the most sense, logically, as I worked with our team; this is really what made the most sense. And we'll be following the process on that."[68]

That Veterans Day, Jim Galloway, the senior political reporter for *The Atlanta Journal-Constitution*, wrote a column about me.

November 11 had special significance for Galloway too. His father, like mine, had enlisted at age seventeen in the Army. Years ago, Jim wrote a thoughtful Veterans Day column about his father and the sacrifice of war, and the newspaper had rerun it online many times through the years.

In 2020, the print version of the paper (the "dead tree edition" as Galloway called it) printed one of his last columns with the headline, "Secretary of state stands up for the facts." He was responding to Monday's letter from Senators Loeffler and Perdue calling for my resignation. He wrote:

> *We tell ourselves that people of character are capable of wondrous things. In fact, more often than not, they simply do ordinary things under extraordinary circumstances. On Monday, Secretary of State Brad Raffensperger stared into a howling tempest—which probably had its origins in the White House—and declared that two plus two equals four. Those who claim the correct answer to be five or three, the Republican said, should be prepared to show their work.* [69]

Galloway had interviewed me on Monday in my office at the capitol at the end of a long afternoon. He quoted me on the heart of the matter:

> *"In these times that we live in, I think it's best to be very mindful of our speech. What people really want at the end of the day—I think both sides should desire honest, fair elections. That's what we've been working for."*

He suggested:

> *The kindest interpretation of Perdue and Loeffler's demand for Raffensperger's head is that they are victims of blackmail, hostages to the Twitter account of a president who, although defeated, still has the power to torpedo their campaigns in 140 characters or less.* [70]

Late Wednesday afternoon, I rode home with Chris, the Georgia patrolman assigned to protect me because of threats. That night Tricia received the first sexualized death threat.

NOVEMBER 12

"THE MOST SECURE ELECTION IN AMERICAN HISTORY"

Tricia reached out to Senators Perdue and Loeffler and asked if they understood what they had unleashed on her and on our family. She sent them each a personal text, and she attached one of the death threats she had received.

On Thursday morning, President Trump tweeted misinformation regarding Dominion Voting Systems machines:

> Must see @seanhannity takedown of the horrible, inaccurate and anything but secure Dominion Voting System which is used in States where tens of thousands of votes were stolen from us and given to Biden. Likewise, the Great @LouDobbs has a confirming and powerful piece![71]

> "REPORT: DOMINION DELETED 2.7 MILLION TRUMP VOTES NATIONWIDE. DATA ANALYSIS FINDS 221,000 PENNSYLVANIA VOTES SWITCHED FROM PRESIDENT TRUMP TO BIDEN. 941,000 TRUMP VOTES DELETED. STATES USING DOMINION VOTING SYSTEMS SWITCHED 435,000 VOTES FROM TRUMP TO BIDEN." @ChanelRion @OANN[72]

I need to emphasize this point: This was not possible—not on a machine-by-machine basis, not by alleged hacking, not by manipulating software, and not by imagined ways of "sending" votes to overseas locations.

We needed help to get factual information out to the public, or else we would be swamped in disinformation. Later that day, the nation's top cybersecurity experts, all the members of the Election Infrastructure Government Coordinating Council (GCC) Executive Committee, said the 2020 election had been "the most secure in American history."[73] Those signing the statement included:

- Cybersecurity and Infrastructure Security Agency (CISA) Assistant Director Bob Kolasky
- U.S. Election Assistance Commission Chair Benjamin Hovland
- National Association of Secretaries of State (NASS) President Maggie Toulouse Oliver
- National Association of State Election Directors (NASED) President Lori Augino
- Escambia County (Florida) Supervisor of Elections David Stafford.

Also signing the statement were the members of the Election Infrastructure Sector Coordinating Council (SCC), which added:

The November 3rd election was the most secure in American history. Right now, across the country, election officials are reviewing and double checking the entire election process prior to finalizing the result.

*When states have close elections, many will recount ballots. All of the states with close results in the 2020 presidential race have paper records of each vote, allowing the ability to go back and count each ballot if necessary. This is an added benefit for security and resilience. This process allows for the identification and correction of any mistakes or errors. **There is no evidence that any voting system deleted or lost votes, changed votes, or was in any way compromised.***

Other security measures like pre-election testing, state certifi-
cation of voting equipment, and the U.S. Election Assistance
Commission's (EAC) certification of voting equipment help to
build additional confidence in the voting systems used in 2020.

While we know there are many unfounded claims and opportunities
for misinformation about the process of our elections, we can assure you
we have the utmost confidence in the security and integrity of our elec-
tions, and you should too. When you have questions, turn to elections
officials as trusted voices as they administer elections.[74]

The statement could not have been clearer and should have put
the issue to rest. Of course, it did not.

NOVEMBER 13

FIRST LAWSUIT AND A CALL FROM SENATOR GRAHAM

On Friday, November 13, counties across the state began the hand
recount of ballots with monitors from state and county party organizations at every location. We encouraged counties to livestream
their recounts when possible to provide maximum transparency.
They provided public viewing areas in addition to allowing designated monitors to stand close to the election workers conducting
the recount. Counties were required to complete their work by
Wednesday, November 18, so we could certify the results two
days later.

Also on Friday, Lin Wood sued me and the Georgia State
Election Board to block certification of the election results. The case
was assigned to Federal District Court Judge Steven D. Grimberg,
who had been appointed by President Trump in April 2019.

Wood argued that procedures in the March 2019 settlement
agreement between the state and the Georgia Democratic Party
might allow invalid ballots to be counted and dilute his own vote.
That, he declared, was unconstitutional.

Later that day, Senator Lindsey Graham (R-SC) called me to ask about our signature match procedure. I didn't understand why Senator Graham would interject himself into a neighboring state's affairs. He seemed to be concerned that some counties might have approved absentee ballot signatures that should have been marked invalid, and he seemed to imply that we could audit all signatures and throw out the ballots from counties that had the highest frequency of error rates. But no state can do that.

It was clear to me that Senator Graham and Lin Wood, both of whom are lawyers, as well as President Trump, were all on the same page, and they didn't understand Georgia's laws regarding absentee ballots.

SIDNEY POWELL: "RELEASE THE KRAKEN"

That night, Trump campaign attorney Sidney Powell appeared on *Lou Dobbs Tonight* and said she could "hardly wait" to reveal "staggering statistical evidence" behind her claims that Venezuela, Cuba, and China were somehow involved through Dominion Voting Systems Corporation to steal the election from Donald Trump. She also claimed that governors and secretaries of state had "financial interests" in the voting machine company, and that they or their families had been enriched because of it.

"I'm going to release the kraken," she said.[75]

The statement left Dobbs momentarily perplexed and soon Powell's announcement became an internet meme representing the insanity, irresponsibility, and legal slander of her statements.

At 7:50 p.m., President Trump tweeted:

> Georgia Secretary of State, a so-called Republican (RINO), won't let the people checking the ballots see the signatures for fraud. Why? Without this the whole process is very unfair and close to meaningless. Everyone knows that we won the state. Where is @BrianKempGA?[76]

NOVEMBER 14

PROFILES IN COURAGE

In the days following the election, as President Trump and some members of my own party attacked me for what I knew was the rule of law, a retired judge from Illinois sent me a copy of John F. Kennedy's *Profiles of Courage*. I had not read the book before, and I was grateful.

In a press interview, I said we needed to go back to school and study our history. *Profiles in Courage* was a great place to start. We all know about four of our greatest leaders—George Washington, Thomas Jefferson, Abraham Lincoln, and Theodore Roosevelt—whose images grace Mount Rushmore. Kennedy's book highlights other great and courageous Americans who have stood in the gap and illuminated a pathway for us to follow. Events thrust those individuals into the spotlight and gave us heroes like Texas icon Sam Houston and Nebraska Senator George Norris.

I opened this book with a quotation from Sam Houston, one of the eight United States senators that Kennedy profiled. The city named for Sam Houston is the nation's fourth most populous. He is also the namesake of Sam Houston National Forest, Sam Houston State University, and the Sam Houston Parkway—all reminders of his giant Texas footprint.

Sam Houston is Texas and Texas is Sam Houston. He heroically led the successful 1836 Battle of San Jacinto that secured Texas's independence from Mexico, and he became the first president of the Republic of Texas. War hero, first and third president of Texas, first U.S. senator from Texas, and then Texas governor.

Houston stood against slavery in the Senate and as Texas governor, and lost both positions soon after those stands.

In 1854 Senator Houston voted against the Kansas-Nebraska Act, which repealed the Missouri Compromise of 1820 and allowed the expansion of slavery into the new territories. The act was supported by his party, the Democrats, and by most of his Texas constituents. Houston chose noble character over a repugnant cause, and the Texas legislature responded in 1857 by refusing to appoint him to another term.

Houston then ran for governor and won. In 1861, he worked in vain to prevent the state from seceding from the Union over the slavery issue. In 1861, the Texas legislature required every office holder to sign an oath of allegiance to the Confederacy. The paper was on his desk to sign. He refused and walked out of his office that day with the paper unsigned. He chose the Union over an unjust cause.

Again, noble character over a cause he could not abide. Leaders lead and sometimes no one follows, even as the leaders stand on sound principles and profound integrity. I wonder today how many Texans who hail Sam Houston's heroics even know this story. How many Americans do? I didn't until I read *Profiles in Courage*.

Sam Houston represents moral courage at its finest. General George S. Patton once said, "Moral courage is the most valuable and usually the most absent characteristic in men." A person of integrity expects to be believed, and when he isn't, he lets time prove him right. Time has proven Sam Houston to have been on the right side of history.

Many organizations dedicated to honor and decency recognize individuals who stand above the crowd. One such organization that holds a high ideal for honor and the rule of law is the National Association of Secretaries of State (NASS), to which I belong.

NASS annually accepts nominations for the organization's highest award, named for Senator Margaret Chase Smith. At the height of McCarthyism in the early 1950s, when Senator Joseph McCarthy was making broad and often false accusations of communist infiltrations throughout American society, Senator Smith spoke on the floor of the Senate and responded with a "Declaration of Conscience":

> *I would like to speak briefly and simply about a serious national condition. The United States Senate has long enjoyed worldwide respect as the greatest deliberative body.... But recently that deliberative character has ... been debased to ... a forum of hate and character assassination.... Freedom of speech is not what it used to be in America.... It has been so abused by some that it is not exercised by others.*[77]

She asked her fellow Republicans not to ride to political victory on the "Four Horsemen of Calumny—Fear, Ignorance, Bigotry, and Smear."

She did not mention Senator McCarthy by name, but he had quietly left the Senate chamber and later tried to ridicule and undercut her.

Four years later, after dozens of innocent Americans had been falsely condemned and blacklisted, the tide finally turned against McCarthy. He was censured by the Senate, and today his name is still synonymous with baseless smear tactics.

To honor Margaret Chase Smith, NASS presents the American Democracy Award in her name for "individual acts of political courage, uncommon character and selfless action in the realm of public service."[78]

Past recipients have included former secretary of state Dr. Condoleezza Rice; Supreme Court Justice Sandra Day O'Connor; former New York Mayor Rudy Giuliani after the 9/11 attack; former Sen. Bob Dole, for the Americans with Disabilities Act; former President Jimmy Carter, for his philanthropic work around the world; civil rights icon Rosa Parks; and many other nationally significant individuals for their specific contributions.

My youngest son, Jay, reminds me, "We can't expect everyone to sacrifice. Some people are too selfish, too stubborn, or just too tired of trying. But it doesn't take everyone. It only takes a few to stand up. Last time a few stood up, more followed them. And those people founded the greatest country on earth."

His generation is watching us.

NOVEMBER 17

"UNSUBSTANTIATED OR TECHNICALLY INCOHERENT"

Chris Krebs, director of the Cybersecurity and Infrastructure Security Agency (CISA) tweeted at 11:45 a.m.:

> ICYMI: On allegations that election systems were manipulated, 59 election security experts all agree, "in every case of which we are aware, these claims either have been unsubstantiated or are technically incoherent." #Protect2020[79]

At 7:07 p.m., President Trump tweeted:

> The recent statement by Chris Krebs on the security of the 2020 Election was highly inaccurate, in that there were massive improprieties and fraud— including dead people voting, Poll Watchers not allowed into polling locations, "glitches" in the voting machines which changed . . . votes from Trump to Biden, late voting, and many more. Therefore, effective immediately, Chris Krebs has been terminated as Director of the Cybersecurity and Infrastructure Security Agency.[80]

FORENSIC AUDIT OF DOMINION EQUIPMENT

And in Georgia, we were just doing our jobs, which in any other year would be of little interest to anyone outside the capitol. Pro V&V (the two Vs stand for verification and validation), an Election Assistance Commission–certified testing laboratory based in

Huntsville, Alabama, completed its post-election review of a random sample of Dominion machines and confirmed there had been no hacking or tampering with the devices.

Pro V&V was not the first to work with us to protect our election. We also partnered with the Department of Homeland Security, the Georgia Cyber Center, Georgia Tech security experts, and other election security experts.

Using forensic techniques, Pro V&V audited a random sample of Dominion Voting Systems voting machines throughout the state. ICP (precinct ballot scanners), ICX (ballot marking devices), and ICC (central absentee ballot scanners) components were all subject to the audit. In conducting the audit, Pro V&V extracted the software or firmware from the components and confirmed all of the software and firmware on the sampled machines was verified to be the software and firmware certified for use by the Office of the Secretary of State.

Coupled with the risk-limiting audit of all paper ballots relying solely on the printed text of the ballots, these steps confirmed the assessment of the Cybersecurity and Infrastructure Security Agency (CISA) that there were no signs of cyberattacks or election hacking and that the machines had accurately recorded the votes cast.

NOVEMBER 18

"YOU CAN TRUST WHAT HE SAYS"

In a story carried across the country, the Associated Press wrote, "Georgia's secretary of state is a man on an island, and the political flood is rising fast as President Donald Trump and his allies vent their outrage at the fellow Republican and make unsupported claims that mismanagement and fraud tainted the state's presidential election."

The AP did mention that I was not completely without support: "Lt. Gov. Geoff Duncan and state House Speaker David Ralston are exceptions: They've joined Kemp in pushing investigations, but have stopped short of attacking Raffensperger."

From former U.S. Senator Saxby Chambliss: "From the standpoint of what I've seen, there just is no widespread fraud in the election process leading up to the general election."

And from my former colleague on the Johns Creek City Council Ivan Figueroa: "There's no hidden agenda. He speaks his mind straight. You can trust what he says."[81]

I had a team in our office of outstanding professionals, some of them with twenty years of experience, who threw themselves in front of this fast-moving freight train for me. They didn't sign up for the onslaught, abuse, and threats, but they redoubled their efforts and worked tirelessly and fearlessly for the people of Georgia to share facts and figures and the truth—the hard truth for Republicans and President Trump that he received fewer votes than Biden.

NOVEMBER 19

RECOUNT CONFIRMS RESULTS

In five days, counties completed the hand count of all the ballots cast in the presidential election. The results upheld and reaffirmed the original outcome produced by the machine tally of votes cast, which was exactly what we expected.

Through the audit process, a few counties identified mistakes made in their original count by not uploading all of the memory cards. Those counties uploaded the memory cards and recertified their results, adding increased accuracy to the results.

The difference between the audit results and the original machine-counted results was well within the expected margin of human error that occurs when hand-counting ballots. The highest error rate in any county recount was 0.73 percent. Most counties found no change in their final tally, and the majority of the remaining counties had changes of fewer than ten ballots.

Deputy Secretary of State Jordan Fuchs established and maintained a partnership with the Carter Center, which has observed more than 110 elections in thirty-nine countries, to provide an impartial assessment of the process. Prior to the election, we had signed a memorandum of understanding with the Carter Center regarding the risk-limiting audit. In the executive summary of its report, the Carter Center noted:

> *Over five days, The Carter Center deployed fifty-two monitors to twenty-five counties. . . . The counties monitored by The Carter Center account for more than 60 percent of votes cast and audited. Completing forms specifically designed for the audit, The Carter Center monitors systematically collected information on each step of the process, including the work of the two-person audit boards and the vote review panels, and the uploading of tally information into the open-source data collection system, Arlo. . . .*

> *Election officials are to be commended for quickly transitioning from an RLA [risk-limiting audit] conducted with a sample of ballots to a full hand tally of all ballots—a risk-limiting audit with a zero risk limit. . . .*

> *The secretary of state and county election officials conducted the RLA in an open and transparent way with rules outlining access and behavior for official party monitors, The Carter Center monitors and public observers. . . .*

> *This report finds that the RLA confirmed the original results of the presidential election in Georgia and commends Georgia election officials for instituting a process that should serve as the basis for increased confidence in the electoral system in the state in the future.*[82]

SIDNEY POWELL: "COMMUNIST MONEY THROUGH VENEZUELA, CUBA, AND LIKELY CHINA"

In a bizarre news conference with fellow Trump campaign attorneys Rudy Giuliani and Jenna Ellis, Sidney Powell said, "What we are really dealing with here and uncovering more by the day is the massive influence of communist money through Venezuela, Cuba and likely China and the interference with our elections here in the United States."[83]

Later, Giuliani said, "The recount being done in Georgia will tell us nothing because these fraudulent ballots will just be counted again because they wouldn't supply the signatures to match the ballots."[84]

I needed to respond, so I used my Facebook page to reply, "Let's address this disinformation about signature match. We strengthened signature match. We helped train election officials on GBI signature match—which is confirmed twice before a ballot is ever cast."[85]

Chris Krebs, who headed the Cybersecurity and Infrastructure Security Agency before he was fired by President Trump, tweeted after the news conference, "That news conference was the most dangerous 1hr 45 minutes of television in American history. And possibly the craziest. If you don't know what I'm talking about, you're lucky."[86]

"NO BASIS IN FACT AND LAW"

That afternoon, after hearing arguments from both sides, Judge Steven D. Grimberg ruled against Lin Wood's emergency request to halt the certification of election results. "To halt the certification at literally the 11th hour would breed confusion and disenfranchisement that I find have no basis in fact and law," Judge Grimberg said from the bench.[87]

NOVEMBER 20

RECOUNT COMPLETE

With the initial machine count and the hand recount completed, we announced certification of the election results on Friday morning. I continued to test negative for COVID-19, so I went downtown to share the news with the media.

"Working as an engineer throughout my life," I said at a capitol press conference, "I live by the motto that numbers don't lie. As secretary of state, I believe that the numbers that we have presented today are correct. The numbers reflect the verdict of the people, not a decision by the secretary of state's office or of courts or of either campaign."[88]

LAWSUIT DISMISSED

Later in the day, Judge Steven D. Grimberg issued his written ruling against Lin Wood, stating that Wood lacked standing in his lawsuit to halt the certification I had just announced. Wood had claimed that the March 2020 settlement agreement between the state of Georgia and the Democratic Party of Georgia had been unconstitutional.

In his ruling, Judge Grimberg wrote:

> Recognizing that Secretary Raffensperger is "the state's chief election official," the General Assembly enacted legislation permitting him (in his official capacity) to "formulate, adopt, and promulgate such rules and regulations, consistent with law, as will be conducive to the fair, legal, and orderly conduct of primaries and elections." The Settlement Agreement is a manifestation of Secretary Raffensperger's statutorily granted authority.[89]

Judge Grimberg added that Wood lacked standing: "The standing inquiry is threefold: The litigant must prove (1) an injury in fact that (2) is fairly traceable to the challenged action of the defendant and (3) is likely to be redressed by a favorable decision." Wood fell short in all three.[90]

"Wood must demonstrate a personal stake in the outcome of the controversy, as a federal court is not a forum for generalized grievances," Judge Grimberg said. "Wood alleges he has standing because he is 'a qualified registered elector residing in Fulton County, Georgia, who has made donations to various Republican candidates on the ballot for the November 3, 2020 elections, and his interests are aligned with those of the Georgia Republican Party for the purposes of the instant lawsuit.' These allegations fall far short of demonstrating that Wood has standing to assert these claims. . . .

"As Wood conceded during oral argument, under his theory any one of Georgia's more than seven million registered voters would have standing to assert these claims. This is a textbook generalized grievance."[91]

The judge also said that if Wood had a claim regarding the settlement agreement, he should have made it earlier. "Nearly eight months later—and after over one million voters cast their absentee ballots in the General Election—Wood challenges the terms of the Settlement Agreement as unconstitutional. Wood could have, and should have, filed his constitutional challenge much sooner than he did, and certainly not two weeks after the General Election. . . .

"CONCLUSION: Wood's motion for temporary restraining order is DENIED."[92]

I had no idea that more than a dozen lawsuits would be filed by President Trump and his supporters over the next two months, many of them related to the signature-match settlement agreement. Every court rejected every claim that the settlement agreement weakened Georgia's signature-match laws.

The agreement came about, as I explained earlier, because Democratic Party groups filed a lawsuit challenging Georgia's signature verification process as unconstitutional. We could have gone to court and won, but the attorney general said that if we were assigned the wrong judge and received a negative ruling, we might lose the ability to use signature match.

So the lawyers negotiated an agreement that called for my office to send out an official election bulletin to every county, outlining best practices for conducting signature verification. The recommended practices were based off many counties' existing procedures. And signature match remained intact—at the absentee ballot application phase and when the actual absentee ballots were returned to the counties. The disinformation and dishonesty on this issue were truly astounding.

MILITIA SHOW UP IN OUR NEIGHBORHOOD

The week before Thanksgiving we heard that a particular anti-government militia organization was planning a rally or something in the street in front of our home. I didn't like the feel of it and thought Tricia and I needed to leave for a few days, but we waited until we heard more. Then on Thursday night I accompanied one of the troopers assigned to our family for security when he and I went to pick up take-out dinner. We had just pulled out of the driveway when Tricia called and said someone had broken into our daughter-in-law's home.

"What?" I asked. "Someone's broken in?"

Hearing only that, the trooper thought Tricia was talking about our home, so he slammed on the brake and threw the car into reverse. At the same time, I saw a car sitting down at the stop sign at the end of the street, and then a pickup truck with an out-of-state tag flew past us. The pickup had been following us, and the trooper's quick reverse threw him for a loop.

Another trooper was at the house with Tricia, and she had a marked car. She drove down to the stop sign where the pickup truck and the other car were sitting. The men inside said they'd heard some Black Lives Matter protesters might be planning something, and they had decided to stick close.

"Oh, really?" she said. "Well, we've got it covered."

The two state troopers were both convinced the two men were who they said they were, but they suspected they were checking out our home and our security.

We are convinced the timing of all that was no coincidence. God placed me in the car with the state trooper, and our daughter-in-law called at just the right time for us to notice those two men and realize the situation was developing quickly.

Tricia and I made arrangements to leave on Friday.

NOVEMBER 21

SIDNEY POWELL: "IT WILL BE BIBLICAL"

The day after the Georgia vote was certified, Sidney Powell appeared on Newsmax to discuss her legal strategy for President Trump. It's likely that this was the interview that led to her dismissal from the president's legal team.

"Georgia's probably going to be the first state I'm gonna blow up," she said. "Mr. Kemp and the secretary of state need to go with it, because they're in on the Dominion scam with their last-minute purchase or award of a contract to Dominion for $100 million. The state bureau of investigation for Georgia ought to be looking into financial benefits received by Mr. Kemp and the secretary of state's family about that time. Another benefit Dominion was created to award was what I call election insurance. That's why Hugo Chavez had it created in the first place. I also wonder where he got the technology, where it actually came from. Because I think it's him or . . . the CIA."

Powell also suggested that Kelly Loeffler's win over Doug Collins was tainted. "We don't know who bought their election," she said. "I'm sure it crosses party lines."

Asked about the lawsuit she planned to file the following week, Powell said, "It will be biblical."[93]

NOVEMBER 22

SIDNEY POWELL DISMISSED

Rudy Giuliani and Jenna Ellis released a statement distancing the Trump team from Powell: "Sidney Powell is practicing law on her own. She is not a member of the Trump Legal Team. She is also not a lawyer for the President in his personal capacity."[94]

Apparently, Powell's Saturday night interview crossed a line of decency for Giuliani. That didn't slow her plan to file a lawsuit in Georgia.

NOVEMBER 25

POWELL RELEASES THE KRAKEN

Tricia and I were on our way home for Thanksgiving when Sidney Powell, no longer working for the Trump campaign, filed her "kraken" lawsuit in federal court. Her bizarre claims were as mythological as the sea creatures they were named for, and even more bizarre than I imagined. I'm amazed that a lawsuit based on a conspiracy can be filed and acted upon by our court system.

"Smartmatic and Dominion were founded by foreign oligarchs and dictators," the lawsuit claimed, "to ensure computerized ballot-stuffing and vote manipulation to whatever level was needed to make certain Venezuelan dictator Hugo Chavez never lost another election."

Dominion, however, is an American company and has no ties to Venezuela.

"As set forth in the accompanying whistleblower affidavit," the lawsuit claimed, "the Smartmatic software was designed to manipulate Venezuelan elections in favor of dictator Hugo Chavez . . ."[95]

Note: Smartmatic is a competitor of Dominion Voting Systems. The state of Georgia had no relationship with Smartmatic. Yet Powell chose to reference false claims about Smartmatic dozens of times in her lawsuit. Not only were her claims lies, they were irrelevant.

She went on for 104 pages, and in the end she asked the court to direct us, among other things, to:

- Decertify the election results.
- Prevent Governor Kemp from transmitting our currently certified results to the Electoral College.
- Require Governor Kemp to reverse the will of Georgia voters and certify election results stating that President Trump won the election.

We were forced to waste taxpayers' resources to answer Powell's kraken claims. If we didn't respond, her lawsuit would go forward. So our legal staff went to work.

And even when we won this court battle, the war over the certification of the election results was not over.

Also on November 25, Lin Wood appealed Judge Grimberg's dismissal of his case to the Eleventh Circuit Court of Appeals. Our legal staff would have to answer that one too.

NOVEMBER 26 – THANKSGIVING DAY

"ENEMY OF THE PEOPLE"

God was so gracious to us. But threats continued to fill our inboxes, and any one of them might have actually been real. We didn't think we should expose our children and grandchildren to unnecessary danger.

We had a quiet Thanksgiving dinner at home with our State Patrol security detail.

President Trump, we learned later, reached out by phone to the armed forces as part of an important holiday tradition for the commander-in-chief to speak to or visit members of the military stationed around the world and away from their families. They sacrifice so much for our safety and to protect our democracy. But the president didn't stop with a simple thank-you. When he hung up the phone, he took a question from someone in the White House press corps in the room with him. "Mr. President, do you have any big plans for your last Thanksgiving in the White House?"

President Trump didn't accept the premise that this might be his last Thanksgiving as president, and he spent the next twenty-five minutes attempting to refute the facts. A reporter asked if voters could have confidence when they cast their votes in the upcoming runoff elections for the U.S. Senate. He answered:

They are tremendous people. Kelly Loeffler, David Perdue are tremendous people. They should be in the United States Senate. They're desperately needed. But I told them today, I said, "Listen, you have a fraudulent system. You have a system with the flick of a switch or the putting in of a new chip can change the course of history, and you have to be very careful."

I read this morning where Stacey Abrams has 850,000 ballots accumulated. Now, that's called harvesting. You're not allowed to harvest, but I understand the Secretary of State who is really, he's an enemy of the people. The Secretary of State, and whether he's Republican or not, this man, what he's done, supposedly he made a deal, and you'll have to check this, where she's allowed to harvest, but in other areas they're not allowed. What kind of a deal is that? They're not allowed to harvest during the presidential.

But how can she say she has 850,000 ballots? That would mean that she's got 850,000 ballots for her. That's not supposed to be happening. That's not an election.[96]

Of course, it didn't happen. It's illegal in Georgia to harvest one ballot. And you can't change a chip and change the course of history. These were the almost daily outrageous claims the president and his allies were making, and all were proven wrong by the evidence and the facts.

In the middle of this harangue, though, Trump crossed another line. He called me "an enemy of the people." It's a phrase once used in Nazi Germany against Jews and in the Soviet Union by Joseph Stalin against anyone who disagreed with him.

How do you respond to that? Who's going to hear? The president had more than 80 million Twitter followers. My Twitter following was smaller than the city of Albany, Georgia.

"PRESERVE, PROTECT, AND DEFEND"

At the capitol, hanging on the wall where I can see it every day, is the oath of office I swore on January 14, 2019:

> *"I do solemnly swear that I will faithfully execute the office of Secretary of State of the state of Georgia and will, to the best of my ability, preserve, protect, and defend the Constitution thereof and the Constitution of the United States."*

I take those words very seriously: " . . . preserve, protect, and defend the Constitution . . ." For all my life, not just as a member of the city council or as secretary of state, but as a citizen of the United States, I considered it my duty and my honor to preserve, protect, and defend the Constitution. Our office follows the Constitution of the state of Georgia, the Constitution of the United States, and the Official Code of Georgia. Everything we do aligns with constitutional provisions and state and federal laws.

Enemy of the people?

Never.

It's an offensive statement.

NOVEMBER 29

"NO MANIPULATION OF THE VOTE"

On Sunday night, *60 Minutes* interviewed Christopher Krebs, former chief of the Cybersecurity and Infrastructure Security Agency (CISA) who told the world, again, what we knew:

I have confidence in the security of this election, because I know the work that we've done for four years in support of our state and local partners. I know the work that the intelligence community has done, the Department of Defense has done, that the FBI has done, that my team has done. I know that these systems are more secure. I know, based on what we have seen, that any attacks on the election were not successful.

That gives you the ability to prove that there was no malicious algorithm or hacked software that adjusted the tally of the vote. And just look at what happened in Georgia. Georgia has machines that tabulate the vote. They then held a hand recount, and the outcome was consistent with the machine vote.

That tells you that there was no manipulation of the vote on the machine count side. And so that, pretty thoroughly in my opinion, debunks some of these sensational claims out there that I've called nonsense and a hoax, that there is some hacking of these election vendors and their software and their systems across the country. It's nonsense.[97]

DECEMBER 1

"SOMEONE'S GOING TO GET KILLED"

Gabe Sterling and Jordan Fuchs were at lunch when Gabe received a phone call reporting that a Dominion contractor had received death threats on Twitter. Gabe quickly scrolled through his Twitter feed and saw the contractor's name and an animated GIF image of a noose slowly swinging back and forth. The man's family was also being threatened.

I didn't realize how angry Gabe was when Jordan called me and said Gabe would like to begin the afternoon press conference with some personal thoughts about the young man. I agreed that would be fine.

When Gabe later stepped up to the podium and ripped off his mask, his face was angry red.

> *Good afternoon. My name is Gabriel Sterling. I'm the voting system implementation manager for the state of Georgia. And just to give y'all a heads up, this is going to be sort of a two-part press conference today. At the beginning of this, I'm going to do my best to keep it together because it has all gone too far. All of it.*
>
> *Joe diGenova* [a Trump campaign lawyer] *today asked for Chris Krebs, a patriot who ran CISA* [the United States Cybersecurity and Infrastructure Security Agency], *to be shot.*
>
> *A twentysomething tech in Gwinnett County today has death threats and a noose put out, saying he should be hung for treason because he was transferring a report on batches from an EMS to a county computer so we could read it.*
>
> *It has to stop. Mr. President, you have not condemned these actions or this language. Senators, you have not condemned this language or these actions. This has to stop. We need you to step up and if you're going to take a position of leadership, show something.*
>
> *My boss, Secretary Raffensperger, his address is out there. They have people doing caravans in front of their house. They've had people come on to their property. Tricia, his wife of forty years, is getting sexualized threats through her cell phone.*
>
> *It has to stop. This is elections. This is the backbone of democracy. And all of you who have not said a damn word are complicit in this. It's too much. Yes. Fight for every legal vote. Go through your due process. We encourage you. Use your First Amendment. That's fine. Death threats, physical threats, intimidation, it's*

too much. It's not right. They've lost the moral high ground to claim that it is.

I don't have all the best words to do this because I'm angry. The straw that broke the camel's back today is again, this twenty-year-old contractor for a voting system company, just trying to do his job. Just there. In fact, I talked to Dominion today and I said, "He's one of the better ones they got." His family is getting harassed now. There's a noose out there with his name on it. That's not right.

I've got police protection outside my house. Fine. I took a higher profile job. I get it. The secretary ran for office. His wife knew that too.

This kid took a job. He just took a job. And it's just wrong. I can't begin to explain the level of anger I have right now over this. And every American, every Georgian, Republican and Democrat alike, should have that same level of anger.

Mr. President, it looks like you likely lost the state of Georgia. We're investigating. There's always a possibility. I get it, and you have the rights to go through the courts.

What you don't have the ability to do, and you need to step up and say this, is stop inspiring people to commit potential acts of violence. Someone's going to get hurt. Someone's going to get shot. Someone's going to get killed. And it's not right. It's not right.

And y'all, I don't have anything scripted. Like I said, I'm going to do my best to keep it together. All of this is wrong.

DiGenova, who said for Chris Krebs to get shot, is a former U.S. attorney. He knows better. The people around the president know better. Mr. President, as the secretary said yesterday, people aren't giving you the best advice of what's actually going on on the ground. It's time to look forward. If you want to run for re-election in four years, fine, do it. But everything we're seeing right now, there's not a path. Be the bigger man here and step in. Tell your supporters, "Don't be violent. Don't intimidate."

All that is wrong. It's un-American.[98]

Gabe was not an elected official, nor was he high profile . . . until that day. But on December 1, his anger was the definition of righteous indignation stepping out from the shadows, and the world listened to him.

Since President Trump began attacking us, I have tried always to speak with calm, measured, deliberate language—not trying to pick battles with anyone. When you're a target, you don't need to inflame people and make yourself a bigger target. Plus, I thought if I cut loose and came out angry, I might not be able control my language as well as Gabe did.

Every time I spoke publicly, I tried to depressurize the situation. Then President Trump or one of his surrogates would go out and spin up the crowd further.

Gabe's comments turned out to be prophetic—people did get killed.

In an example of the president's surrogates spinning up the crowd, earlier Thursday morning, Trump's attorney Lin Wood had tweeted that the president should declare martial law:

> **Good morning.**
> Our country is headed to civil war. A war created by
> 3rd party bad actors for their benefit – not for We The
> People.
> Communist China is leading the nefarious efforts to
> take away our freedom.@realDonaldTrump should
> declare martial law.[99]

U.S. ATTORNEY GENERAL: "WE HAVE NOT SEEN FRAUD"

U.S. Attorney General William Barr told the Associated Press, "To date, we have not seen fraud on a scale that could have effected a different outcome in the election."[100]

Barr was one of President Trump's strongest defenders and the man at the top of the Department of Justice, and he stated the truth clearly and definitively.

Once again, the case should be closed. Yet it was not. Not by a long shot.

DECEMBER 2

TRUMP: "SHOW SIGNATURES"

Overnight President Trump tweeted:

> Rigged Election. Show signatures and envelopes. Expose the massive voter fraud in Georgia. What is Secretary of State and @BrianKempGA afraid of. They know what we'll find!!![101]

DECEMBER 3

STATE SENATE HEARINGS

On December 3, two committees of the Georgia State Senate held hearings on the election—the Government Affairs Committee and a subcommittee of the Judiciary Committee (which is composed primarily of lawyers). The Government Affairs Committee, chaired by Senator Bill Heath, sought answers to questions being raised by President Trump and others since Election Day. He began with an introduction:

> *After a number of alleged improprieties were brought to our atten-*
> *tion following the general election on November 3, I, as well as*

every member of this committee, have received numerous questions and concerns about the security of our elections. And we have all heard potentially troublesome anecdotes from concerned citizens across the state.

. . . The purpose of today's meeting is to hear firsthand account from election officials from across the state in order to establish the appropriate context for the stories we've heard.

While all of us can easily speculate what is and what is not abnormal during an election, I thought it best to hear from the experts who have dedicated considerable amount of their livelihoods to administering elections. While we certainly won't have time to address each and every story shared with us, I hope that by learning more about the process and highlighting a few of the major issues, we'll be better equipped to make a determination about what exactly happened on Election Day.[102]

The hearing was similar to the thousands of other hearings held in the capitol throughout the decades—though a little longer than usual at three hours—with senators seeking to better understand the answers to the questions they were hearing from their constituents. Here are sample exchanges:

Senator Tyler Harper: On the ballot drop boxes, is there a verifiable chain of custody from the time that box is picked up, taken to the warehouse or wherever it is taken to, until that ballot box is opened to be counted?

Ryan Germany: Yes. So the regulation requires that at least two people who were sworn deputy registrars pick up those ballots, count them, put them in a sealed container, fill out a chain of custody form, and deliver it to the county elections office. At that point, they confirm the number of ballots, and then fill out the chain of custody form that has been delivered.

Senator Harper: So at that time that that is done, we know how many ballots are in that drop box when it is taken to that place. So there is a count of those number of ballots at that particular time.

Germany: Correct.

Senator Harper: Okay. So regardless of how long it may take us to count ballots, we know how many ballots we may or may not be counting in the next couple of hours during that time period. Is that—

Germany: So, for drop boxes, yes, that's correct. And you're talking about for when they close them up at 7:00 p.m. on election night because they're emptying them every day and bringing them in. On election night, to be able to have that count. And then there's also ones that come in to the office by that time, 7:00 p.m., just through the mail process. There would not be a count on those, but they would be counted as well.

Sen. Steve Gooch: The voting machines, when you go in and you punch on the touch screens that I'm going to vote for a president candidate A or B, do any of those machines have any connectivity to the internet?

Germany: No.

Senator Gooch: Do they have a USB connectivity?

Germany: They have a USB connectivity in the sense that that's how the machines are loaded, but then that's sealed prior to when they're in use. So no one has access to it.

Senator Gooch: So do those machines get used to tabulate the votes or is it just through the scanner?

Germany: The touchscreens are just used to print a piece of paper. That's it.

Senator Gooch: And then when you take the ballot over to the scanner and you scan it, can it spit the ballot back out and then you put it back in again or does it go in and drop in?

Germany: Yes sir.

Senator Gooch: Okay. So my personal experience is that once it goes in, it drops down. It doesn't come back out.

Germany: Correct.

Senator Gooch: I've been told there's cases where the ballots have been rejected multiple times and they go back in, come back out, and go back in and that some of those machines could be programmed to count those multiple times.

Germany: So there's been allegations of that in Michigan, I think I just saw, or maybe it was Arizona, one of these other states. So one thing that I think was good about Secretary Raffensperger ordering the audit of the presidential election, the fact that the hand count of each ballot almost exactly matched the machine count proves that didn't happen.

Senator Gooch: Thank you.[103]

GIULIANI'S SLICED-AND-DICED VIDEO

In the afternoon, Senator William Ligon chaired a Senate Judiciary subcommittee hearing for seven hours, where Rudy Giuliani and other lawyers for President Trump presented witnesses and a video that had been deceptively sliced and edited so that it appeared to show the exact opposite of reality.

In the days and nights following the election, election workers were tabulating ballots at State Farm Arena, and Fulton County kept multiple security cameras rolling nonstop. Video images from Tuesday night showed workers, when they were told they would go home for the night, following Georgia law and regulations by placing all of the uncounted ballots into official boxes and sealing them so they could not be tampered with. Then they put the boxes under the tables where they had been working.

Media representatives remained in the room and were visible on the video.

When I got word that they were stopping for the night at just 10:30, I sent word asking that they continue counting. So they went back to work, and forty minutes later they bought out the same official boxes, unsealed them, and began counting again.

There can be no mistaking of the facts. Giuliani knows this.

Yet he sat before members of the Georgia State Senate and showed a slice of video that had removed the clear evidence that Fulton County election workers had protected the ballots and the process as required by law.

"When you look at what you saw on the video," Giuliani said, "which to me was a smoking gun, powerful smoking gun, well, I don't have to be a genius to figure out what happened. I don't have to be a genius to figure out that those votes are not legitimate votes."[104]

Giuliani intentionally misled our senators. He has yet to stand before a judge in Georgia with the same "evidence" and make the same claim. He knows that doing so would put at risk his license to practice law. Attorneys are bound to tell the truth in court. New York's highest court would later suspend Giuliani's license to practice law, based in large part on his intentional spreading of misinformation about the election in Georgia.

Within hours of the hearing with Giuliani's chopped-up video, online conspiracy theorists had identified one of the election workers, posted her name online, and claimed "she was involved in voter fraud on a MASSIVE SCALE." She and her daughter, who also worked for Fulton County, became unsuspecting targets of thousands more conspiracy theorists, and eventually President Trump, who would make them a major talking point in our phone conversation a month later.

These two women did nothing wrong. They were two people among thousands nationwide who work long, long hours on Election Day to support our democracy.

DECEMBER 4

THE SETTLEMENT AGREEMENT, A.K.A., "CONSENT DECREE"

Here's a brief, but important, civics lesson:

The legislative branch of government passes laws.

The chief executive—the governor—signs laws.

The executive branch carries out the laws, often creating regulations that clarify and interpret those laws.

The Office of the Secretary of State is part of Georgia's executive branch, and as such, it creates regulations through the State Election Board administrative rules and regulations that are consistent with the laws passed by the legislature and signed by the governor.

I begin with that explanation because in November 2020, President Trump began a Twitter tirade against Georgia's absentee ballot signature-match procedure, and got it "flat out, 100 percent, four square wrong," as Gabe Sterling so eloquently put it.[105]

The president tweeted:

> The Consent Decree signed by the Georgia Secretary of State, with the approval of Governor @BrianKempGA, at the urging of @staceyabrams, makes it impossible to check & match signatures on ballots and envelopes, etc. They knew they were going to cheat. Must expose real signatures![106]

Everything in that statement is wrong, including the main point. Signature match is required by state law and was not weakened or stopped. In fact, we actually strengthened signature matching in 2020 and even made GBI signature-match identification training available for county election officials. Signature matching was performed twice: at the absent ballot application phase and when the signed absentee ballot with its envelope with the voter's signature was returned to the election office.

Yet immediately, many Republicans—including dozens of Republican Georgia lawmakers—fell into lockstep with President Trump's mischaracterization.

In fact, in 2019, the Republicans lawmakers had passed House Bill 316, which said this about signature match:

In order to be found eligible to vote an absentee ballot by mail, the registrar or absentee ballot clerk shall compare the identifying information on the application with the information on file in the registrar's office and, if the application is signed by the elector, compare the signature or mark of the elector on the application with the signature or mark of the elector on the elector's voter regis-tration card. . . .

*If the elector has failed to sign the oath, or if the signature does not appear to be valid, or if the elector has failed to furnish required information or information so furnished does not conform with that on file in the registrar's or clerk's office, or if the elector is other-wise found disqualified to vote, the registrar or clerk shall write across the face of the envelope "Rejected," giving the reason there-fore. The board of registrars or absentee ballot clerk shall **promptly notify** the elector of such rejection, [emphasis added] . . .[107]*

In November 2019, the Democratic Party of Georgia sued the secretary of state seeking to eliminate signature match completely. That was not going to happen.

Attorney Vincent R. Russo represented our office in court along with the Georgia attorney general. Russo had been general counsel for the secretary of state's office until he went into private practice, and he continued to represent us in several cases, including

Curling v. Kemp (later *v. Crittenden*, later *v. Raffensperger*). Russo is also the general counsel for the Georgia Republican Party, and he has represented the National Republican Congressional Committee.

Russo and the attorney general did a great job of negotiating an agreement in which we simply followed Georgia law as passed by the legislature in HB 316, and the Democratic Party withdrew its lawsuit and released any claims regarding Georgia's signature-matching laws, meaning they could not try to assert those claims again later in the election cycle or after the 2020 election.

The General Assembly had left the term "promptly notify" undefined in the statute, leaving that detail to the State Election Board. In a regulation passed in the normal course of its business, the State Election Board defined "promptly notify" as "no later than the close of business on the third business day after receiving the absentee ballot." If the ballot was rejected in the last week before the election, then "promptly notify" meant "no later than close of business on the next business day."

Our office also issued an Official Election Bulletin to counties offering guidance for rejecting an absentee ballot for a mismatched signature:

> *If the registrar or absentee ballot clerk determines that the voter's signature on the mail-in absentee ballot envelope does not match any of the voter's signatures on file in eNet* [Georgia's voter registration system] *or on the absentee ballot application, the registrar or absentee ballot clerk must seek review from two other registrars, deputy registrars, or absentee ballot clerks. A mail-in absentee ballot shall not be rejected unless a majority of the registrars, deputy registrars, or absentee ballot clerks reviewing the signature agree that the signature does not match any of the voter's signatures on file in eNet or on the absentee ballot application.*[108]

President Trump is not a lawyer, and he completely misunder-stood—or was misled by his advisors—everything about the settle-ment agreement. Everything.

Even though the Georgia Attorney General's office (led by Republican Chris Carr) had expressly recommended that we enter into the settlement, the Republican Party of Georgia claimed, "The Consent Decree exceeded Respondents' authority under the Georgia Constitution," and "the Consent Decree is unauthorized under Georgia law and is therefore null and void." And they asked the court to "issue a declaratory judgment that the Consent Decree violates the Constitution of the state of Georgia and the laws of the state of Georgia."[109] A settlement agreement their own general counsel had signed!

COURTS: THE ULTIMATE FACT-CHECK

The Trump–Shafer–Republican Party filed a lawsuit in Fulton County Superior Court in an attempt to prevent certification of the election results in Georgia, prevent me as secretary of state from my lawful duty of appointing Georgia's electors to the Electoral College, and ordered a new presidential election in Georgia.

In the weeks and months after the election, multiple media organizations fact-checked the claims made by President Trump, his legal team, and others. The ultimate fact-check in the United States, however, occurs in courts of law, where witnesses swear to tell the truth or risk imprisonment and where lawyers must also tell the truth or risk disbarment.

If you want to know the truth, watch what happens in court.

WSB-TV INVESTIGATIVE REPORTER REVIEWS VIDEO

Gabe Sterling asked Justin Gray, an investigative reporter with WSB-TV in Atlanta, to review the uncut security tape of State Farm Arena. Afterward, Gray tweeted:

I just spent 2 hours going through State Farm surveillance video with @GabrielSterling & state investigators. We watched chain of custody of the table & ballot boxes in question - from 8am until midnight. The boxes were packed & sealed with observers in room - nothing improper.[110]

Below an image of secure cases to hold ballots, he tweeted:

if you are someone who doesn't even believe the simple, basic fact (that has nothing to do with anything) that these are not suitcases - you live in a world outside of reason & reality. Here they are loading the crates - while observers and media were in the room at 10:01pm.[111]

DECEMBER 5

COURT OF APPEALS: WOOD LACKS STANDING

The ruling by the Eleventh Circuit Court of Appeals may have been Lin Wood's last stand:

We agree with the district court that Wood lacks standing to sue because he fails to allege a particularized injury. And because Georgia has already certified its election results and its slate of presidential electors, Wood's requests for emergency relief are moot to the extent they concern the 2020 election. The Constitution makes clear that federal courts are courts of limited jurisdiction, U.S. Const. art. III ; we may not entertain post-election contests about garden-variety issues of vote counting and misconduct that may properly be filed in state courts.[112]

DECEMBER 6

RUMOR WHACK-A-MOLE

County officials in south Georgia were forced to fact-check Representative Jody Hice (R-GA), when the congressman tweeted flat-out misinformation that generated national news. On December 4, Hice tweeted:

> Yesterday we learned a forensics examination of a Ware County, GA #DominionVotingSystems machine found votes were switched from @realDonaldTrump to @JoeBiden.[113]

The fake story, which included false claims that Ware County machines were "seized," generated significant traffic on social media, and national news organizations followed up.

Ware County Election Supervisor Carlos Nelson debunked the misinformation for *Politico:* "I can tell you this is—I don't want to cuss—this is a darned lie. Our vote machines are secure. There's no vote-flips."[114] He also stated the obvious: no Ware County equipment was seized.

And add to that, Ware County voted 69.8 percent for President Trump.

Nelson said that an elections worker made a thirty-seven-vote tabulation error on election night, and the mistake was discovered during an internal audit. The voting machines were not involved.

"There was no vote flipping," Nelson said. "The system worked like it should."[115]

Walter Jones, a conservative former journalist who was my office's communications manager for voter education responded, "This is another of the falsehoods being pedaled by conspiracy advocates trying to convince the gullible of why the presidential election didn't turn out as they'd hoped. No voting machines have been seized. No one has unearthed evidence of 'vote flipping' because it didn't happen. And no one has discovered some secret algorithm for altering the election outcome because that's nonsense."[116]

DECEMBER 7

ANTI-DISINFORMATION MONDAY

At a morning press conference at the Capitol, Gabe Sterling and I attempted to straighten out some of the disinformation Rudy Giuliani and others had fomented on Thursday. I told the media:

> *All this talk of a stolen election, whether it's Stacey Abrams or the President of the United States, is hurting our state. The vast majority of Georgians, Republicans and Democrats, want us, all of us as elected officials to focus on protecting and growing Georgia jobs, getting the* [COVID-19] *vaccine out as efficiently as possible and getting back to normal. The focus on November 3 is drawing energy away from those goals. The president has his due process rights, and those are available to him. It's time we all focus on the future and growth. I know there are people that are convinced the election was fraught with problems, but the evidence, the actual evidence, the facts tell us a different story.*[117]

Gabe, exasperated at having to punch down more lies, this time about Giuliani's sliced-up video, said,

> *What you saw, the "secret suitcases"* [with Gabe's air quotes] *with magic ballots, were actually ballots that had been packed into those absentee ballot carriers by the workers in plain view of the monitors and the press. The reason they were packed away is because they were under the misbegotten impression that they were getting to go home. Which, if you notice when you go back to see the videos on this, they were packing these things up 10:00, 10:30 at night. You see some of the same people*

there at 7:00 and 7:30 and 8:00 in the morning setting up those tables. They had been there all day long. They were tired and wanted to go home and they thought they could. . . . then you see Ralph Jones at State Farm Arena getting a phone call around that time, as he's literally with blue seals in his hand to seal up these containers and you can see his shoulders kind of slump for a second. Then he goes over and does some more work on the side. I think getting up the courage to go tell these workers who had been there all day, "Hey guys, we have to stay here longer to keep scanning at least the batches we have." So you could watch all this happen. You can see it from the beginning to the end.[118]

For eighteen minutes Gabe addressed disinformation and conspiracy theories, such as:

Let's be clear, there was no water main break. There was a urinal that they turn off during the downtime at State Farm because there's no events going on there. And it had a little slow leak that came over the side. . . . You will see [in the video] *the Zamboni little carpet drier thingy driving around. I mean, you can see all the things happening.*

There are no seized machines in Ware County. Not true, did not happen. There was a written report from an activist who says the hand count was thirty-seven off, it was. He says, "The only reason it could be off is because of an algorithm in the machines." Which is ridiculous. What have we been saying since the beginning, the most obvious fault point in any of the system is the human beings who were counting them. Again, it was 0.26 percent.

[State Sen.] *Jen Jordan and* [State Sen.] *Elena Parent did not get on a plane to go count votes in Pennsylvania, okay? They basically said, "Here's a picture of a blonde woman in a mask. Here's another picture of a blonde woman in a mask. Obviously the conspiracy where Democrat state senators are counting ballots in Pennsylvania." It's ridiculous. I can't believe I just keep on standing here and saying these things, but I do.*

There is no algorithm, the 5 million ballot hand-count proves there's no algorithm switching votes. Is there any of the disinformation I missed over the weekend guys? I'm not sure.[119]

JUDGE DISMISSES POWELL LAWSUIT

Judge Timothy C. Batten dismissed Sidney Powell's "kraken" lawsuit on Monday. "They want this court to substitute its judgment for the 2.5 million voters who voted for Biden," the judge wrote. "This I'm unwilling to do."[120]

The ruling was important for election integrity in Georgia and across the country. When I heard of the court's decision, I said, "Georgians can now move forward knowing that their votes, and only their legal votes, were counted accurately, fairly, and reliably."

RECOUNT RESULTS CERTIFIED

Our office also certified the recount results Monday, even as we continued to fend off further allegations of widespread voting fraud in Georgia.

At a capitol press conference, I said, "It's been a long thirty-four days since the election on November 3. We have now counted legally cast ballots three times, and the results remain unchanged. Continuing to make debunked claims of stolen elections is hurting our state."[121]

DECEMBER 8

TEXAS V. GEORGIA

The state of Texas sued the state of Georgia on December 8, and sixteen Georgia state senators applauded.

Texas Attorney General Ken Paxton wrote in the lawsuit that went directly to the U.S. Supreme Court, "Trust in the integrity of our election processes is sacrosanct and binds our citizenry and the states in this union together."[122]

Then he claimed, "Georgia, Michigan, Pennsylvania, and Wisconsin destroyed that trust and compromised the security and integrity of the 2020 election."[123]

Specifically, Texas claimed without evidence that 80,000 absentee ballots with forged signatures had been submitted and accepted in Georgia.

Thirteen of Georgia's Republican state senators, along with three state senators elect, signed a statement applauding Texas "for recognizing that the failure of the state of Georgia to follow its own election laws has violated the Equal Protection Act of the U.S. Constitution.... We urge the U.S. Supreme Court to accept this very important case submitted last night by the State of Texas."[124]

Georgia's attorney general, in a brief opposing Texas, stated the obvious:

> *This election cycle, Georgia did what the Constitution empowered it to do: it implemented processes for the election, administered the election in the face of logistical challenges brought on by COVID-19, and confirmed and certified the election results— again and again and again.*
>
> *Yet Texas has sued Georgia anyway . . .*
>
> *. . . Contrary to Texas' argument, Georgia has exercised its powers under the Electors Clause. Georgia's legislature enacted laws governing elections and election disputes, and the State and its officers have implemented and followed those laws.*[125]

DECEMBER 9

UNITED STATES V. GEORGIA?

A day later, President Trump suggested with a tweet that his campaign or the federal government would in some way join Texas in its lawsuit.

> We will be INTERVENING in the Texas (plus many other states) case. This is the big one. Our Country needs a victory!
> — Donald J. Trump (@realDonaldTrump) December 9, 2020[126]

DECEMBER 10

MORE DISINFORMATION AND ANOTHER LAWSUIT

A committee of the Georgia House of Representatives scheduled a hearing with Rudy Giuliani and other election conspiracy-mongers. The state was facing several lawsuits filed against it by the invitees, and I determined it was prudent not to participate.

Every time Giuliani and his team stepped up to a microphone and offered further disinformation, it was like the rumor Whack-a-Mole all over again. We addressed this one, and we had a transparent process, and we had press releases on a daily basis, and then another false claim popped up over there. It was literally impossible for my office to keep up with and respond to the misinformation and outright lying. The election conspiracy theorists created new fake stories faster than anybody could respond with fact.

As Gabe Sterling said at a press conference, "Giving oxygen to this continued disinformation is leading to a continuing erosion of people's belief in our elections and our processes."[127]

Meanwhile, our investigators had opened 132 investigations into complaints of potential voting violations statewide. They were seeing typical post-election issues, but no evidence of widespread fraud or anything to suggest that the results were not accurate.

DECEMBER 11

SCOTUS REJECTS TEXAS

The U.S. Supreme Court refused to hear the Texas case. In a short, unsigned order, the Court wrote, "Texas has not demonstrated a judicially cognizable interest in the manner in which another State conducts its elections. All other pending motions are dismissed as moot."[128] None of the three justices appointed by President Trump supported Texas's position.

On the same day, Georgia House of Representatives Speaker David Ralston, angry with me for not participating in the hearing the day before, said he would move to take away Georgia citizens' ability to elect their secretary of state and give that power to the state legislature.

The speaker made it clear that his motivation was because he didn't like the way I was doing my job. He mentioned the settlement agreement negotiated and signed by the attorney general in March 2020 (Ralston incorrectly called it a "consent decree"—a serious error for a lawyer who should know the difference). He also said he disagreed with my decision to mail absentee ballot request forms without asking permission of the legislature. And finally, he was upset that my office did not participate in the circus hearing in the House.

"As the state's chief elections official," he told the media, "it is incumbent on the secretary of state to be responsive to the People's House and faithfully perform his or her duties in accordance with the laws passed by the General Assembly."[129]

Of course, I did perform my duties in accordance with the Georgia Constitution and the laws of our state; however, as a constitutional officer of the state of Georgia, I am elected by the people, and my responsibility is to the people of Georgia.

The speaker said he would prefer for the legislature to appoint a bureaucrat as secretary of state—someone beholden to the legislature.

The people of Georgia don't want to give up their power to elect the secretary of state, and the speaker's attempted power grab went nowhere. Months later, during the 2021 General Assembly, the Senate passed Senate Bill 202, which addressed the mailing of absentee ballots. The House took up SB202 and substituted a more comprehensive bill to revise elections and voting. The substitute bill created for the first time measures for the State Election Board (SEB) to hold counties accountable for their management of elections. That accountability measure was a good thing and long overdue.

However, the substitute bill also removed the secretary of state as chair of the SEB and instead made the secretary a nonvoting ex-officio member of the board. I can only assume this change was directed at me by the speaker of the house. Whatever his reason, personal politics or otherwise, the impact reaches far beyond my relationship with the speaker in ways that are impossible to predict.

From a practical standpoint, as chair of the board, the secretary of state can respond much quicker to a habitually wayward county that has had long-enduring, gross mismanagement and dysfunction.

The General Assembly removed from the voters and gave itself the authority to elect the chair of the SEB, but then adjourned and left town without electing a new chair.

Meanwhile, in the summer of 2021, when voters were clamoring for the SEB to take action against Fulton County election mismanagement, the speaker of the house conveniently never told those irate voters he never filled that position.

DECEMBER 14

SENATORS' PRESS RELEASE MISSES THE MARK

On the same day that early voting began for their January 5 runoffs, Senators Loeffler's and Perdue's campaigns appeared to be more concerned about pressuring me than running their campaigns. Or perhaps pressuring me was part of their campaign. Whatever the reason, it didn't go well for them.

The senators collaborated on another press release and demanded information that was already available to the public and that their campaigns had received from the National Republican Senatorial Committee (NRSC).

It started on Monday, when the senators released a joint statement to the media insisting that I release the list of individuals who had registered to vote in Georgia since the November 3 election:

> *It's been one week since the voter registration deadline passed and the Secretary of State has failed to compile and release a final list of newly registered voters. This is totally unacceptable—the deadline for new voter registration was December 7, 2020.*

> *In-person early voting starts today, and the public remains without a full accounting of who is registered and who may attempt to cast a ballot in the runoff. This lack of transparency needs to be rectified immediately, or the integrity of our elections will remain threatened.*

> *Georgians demand transparency, accountability, and accuracy in our elections process—and the Secretary of State is failing to provide it in a timely manner.*[130]

In fact, each day since the election, the NRSC had requested and received from my office the updated lists of the newly registered Georgia voters—the very list that Loeffler and Perdue insisted our office had "failed to compile and release."

The Georgia voter list has been a core part of effective Georgia political campaigns, allowing campaigns and outside groups to target voters for turnout or messaging. Concerned after hearing in the media that the senators did not have the data, our office reached out to the NRSC, which confirmed that it had shared that public data with the Perdue and Loeffler senate campaigns.

ACCOUNTABILITY AND TRANSPARENCY: ANOTHER UPDATE

We were wearing a groove into the marble floor at the capitol from my office to the foot of the steps where we met the media almost daily. Our frequent press conferences were an important part of our effort to maintain transparency. Shine a light on every aspect of the process, and people can see the truth with their own eyes.

Like many of these updates, I began the Monday conference visit by reminding the media that Georgia's elections are secure. "There are many telling you they aren't," I said. "I supported and voted for the president, and I am sorely disappointed in the outcome like millions and millions of other Americans. But we have over 200 years of transitions of power in our nation, regardless of personality, regardless of party. In the past few weeks, partisans have asked that I choose party above law. That's not going to happen. My loyalty is to God, our Constitution, and our nation."[131]

We announced we would begin a signature-match audit in Cobb County, partnering with the Georgia Bureau of Investigation to confirm the authenticity of thousands of signatures. We selected Cobb County for the signature audit because it was the only county where the president and his allies had submitted credible evidence that the signature-verification process had not been conducted properly.

Conducting the audit did not in any way suggest that Cobb County was not properly following election procedures or properly conducting signature matching.

We also partnered with the University of Georgia on a state-wide signature-match review. The UGA School of Public and International Affairs would study a sample of signed envelopes from each county from the presidential election. It was intended to be

forward-looking, helping to inform and optimize election administration for future elections.

GEORGIA'S ELECTORS CAST THEIR VOTES

In the Senate chamber of the Georgia capitol, the state's sixteen
Electoral College electors cast their votes for Joe Biden. Likewise,
around the country, electors cast their votes, 306 for Biden and 232
for Trump.

The votes would be delivered to Washington, D.C., for certification on January 6, 2021.

DECEMBER 23

TRUMP CALLS SOS INVESTIGATOR

President Trump had Georgia signatures on his mind two days
before Christmas. The Georgia Bureau of Investigation (GBI) was
still conducting an audit of more than 15,000 signatures in Cobb
County. The president tweeted:

> They are slow walking the signature verification in
> Georgia. They don't want results to get out prior to
> January 6th. They know what they are trying so hard
> to hide. Terrible people! @BrianKempGA[132]

Later that same day, President Trump called Frances Watson, the
lead investigator in our office, and asked her to do his bidding, telling her:

*So I won Florida in a record number, Ohio in a record, Texas in
a record, Alabama by 40, 40 points. And I won everything but
Georgia and, you know and I won Georgia, I know that, by a lot
and the people know it.*

*And you know something happened, I mean, something bad
happened. And I hope you join that* [unintelligible]. *You know
I hope you're going back two years, as opposed to just checking you*

know one against the other, because that would be a signature check that didn't mean anything.

But if you go back two years, and if you can get to Fulton, you're going to find things that are gonna be unbelievable, the dishonesty that we've heard from them.[133]

President Trump was giving Frances instructions on how to conduct a signature audit, although it was actually the GBI and the secretary of state investigators conducting a joint audit. He wanted the audit to be conducted in Fulton County, though nobody had been accused of voting improperly in Fulton.

"But Fulton," President Trump said, "Fulton is the mother lode, you know, as the expression goes, Fulton County—"

"Well, Mr. President," Frances said, "right, yeah, I appreciate your comments, and I can assure you that our team and the GBI . . . that we're only interested in the truth and finding—"

"Right, that's great."

"And finding the information that's based on the facts, and you know we've been working twelve sixteen-hour days."

"Great."

"And we're working through it," Frances said, "and so I can assure you that, and I do appreciate you calling I know you're a very busy, very important man, and I'm very honored that you called. And you know quite—"

"It's so important what you're doing."[134]

Frances may have thought the call was ending there, but the president continued uninterrupted.

Mark asked me to do it. He thinks you're great, and you know, just you have the most important job in the country right now, because if we win Georgia, first of all, if we win you're going to have two wins . . . They're not gonna win right now, you know, they're down because the people of Georgia are so angry at what happened to me. They know I won, won by hundreds of thousands of votes. It wasn't close. And Alabama you know where they go, because I won South Carolina in a record, Alabama in a record, Florida in a record. You know I won Florida by six or seven hundred thousand votes. It's never happened before with a Republican. And with all that money they spent, you know, you heard all about these guys go down spending a fortune. And we won Texas by a record, Texas was won by the biggest, biggest number ever. And it, you know, it didn't, it didn't . . . And Ohio, of course, you know that you know about that. That was won by nine points or something, And it's . . . all of it. Iowa, I mean. And it didn't—it never made sense and, you know, they dropped ballots. They dropped all these ballots. Stacey Abrams—really really terrible, I mean just a terrible thing . . . And I will say this, if and when, I mean hopefully, this will show because if you go back two years or four years, you're going to see it's a totally different signature. But hopefully, you know, I will, when—when the right answer comes out you'll be praised. I don't know why they made it so hard, they will be praised. People will say, "Great!" Because that's what it's about, that ability to check and, and to make it right. Because everyone knows it's wrong. There's just no way. You know they had people in Georgia, for instance, that won, and I was way ahead of them, and they won because of me, you know, I pulled them, as they call it coattails, right, and we pulled them across. And they say, "There's no way that I beat you by fifteen points." You know I've had that, we've had plenty of those calls too so. Anyway, but whatever you can do Frances, It would be—It's a great thing, it's an important thing for the country, so important. You have no idea, so important, and I very much appreciate it.[135]

DECEMBER 29

GBI SIGNATURE AUDIT: NO FRAUDULENT BALLOTS

The Georgia Bureau of Investigation experts examined the signatures on 15,118 ballot oath envelopes from randomly selected boxes in Cobb County and found "no fraudulent absentee ballots." Only two ballots should have been identified by Cobb County Elections Officials for cure notification that weren't. In one case, the ballot was "mistakenly signed by the elector's spouse," and in the other, the voter "reported signing the front of the envelope only."[136] In both cases, the identified voters filled out the ballots themselves.

The audited signatures represented 10 percent of the 150,431 absentee ballots received by Cobb County elections officials during the November election, enough for a 99 percent confidence interval in the results of the audit.

The signature audit represented the third strike against voter fraud claims in Georgia.

Our office conducted a statewide hand recount that reaffirmed the initial tally and a machine recount at the request of the Trump campaign that also reaffirmed the original tally. The signature audit disproved the only credible allegations the Trump campaign had against the strength of Georgia's signature match processes.

To conduct the audit, law enforcement officers from GBI and the secretary of state's office were instructed to "analyze and compare the known signatures, markings, and identifying information of the elector as stored in databases with the signature, markings, and identifying information on the elector's ABM ballot oath envelope." They looked for "distinctive characteristics and unique qualities . . . individual attributes of the signature, mark, or other identifying information" to "make a judgment of the validity of the signature on each envelope based on the totality of the documents."[137]

The law enforcement officers conducting the audit were split into eighteen two-member teams, identified as "inspection teams" and two three-member teams identified as "investigation teams." If the members of an inspection team were split on whether a ballot signature was valid, a third impartial "referee" was brought in to break the tie. This only happened on six occasions.

In cases where an additional review was necessary, if no signature was on the ballot, or if additional identification documents were not available, the absentee ballots were given to the investigation teams to track down more information.

The inspection teams submitted 396 envelopes to the investigation teams for comparison with additional documents or follow-up with the elector, and 386 of those were accepted as valid. The remaining ten were referred for additional investigation. "All ten electors were located, positively identified, and interviewed."[138]

The law enforcement officers used the Cobb County elections database, which included signature information from voter registration forms, absentee ballot applications, voter certificates, passports, and certificates of naturalization, in addition to other documents.

The Cobb County Elections Department had "a 99.99% accuracy rate in performing correct signature verification procedures."[139]

TRUMP: "NOBODY CAN BE THIS STUPID"

A few minutes before midnight, the president tweeted:

> I love the great state of Georgia, but the people who run it, from the Governor, @BrianKempGA, to the Secretary of State, are a complete disaster and don't have a clue, or worse. Nobody can be this stupid. Just allow us to find the crime, and turn the state Republican.[140]

> Now it turns out that Brad R's brother works for
> China and they definitely don't want "Trump". So
> disgusting![141]

This was unequivocally not true. Conspiracy-theory websites had falsely claimed that the chief technology officer for the Chinese company Huawei, Ron Raffensperger, was my brother, and the president amplified the lie with his tweet. I don't have a brother named Ron and, for the record, none of my family works for China or for any Chinese company. I learned after the tweet that a man with the same last name as mine worked for the Chinese company Huawei, but despite having the same last name, he is not my brother and we have never met. I hope his life has returned to normal. Even today, that rumor still persists in the ether of the social media world.

DECEMBER 30

"MASTER PITCHMAN" IS A FAILED TREASURE HUNTER

"What do you do once you've bilked companies such as the Belo Corp., Radio Shack, Young & Rubicam, and Coca-Cola of investments between $10 million and $37.5 million for a product that flops? You change your name," *FastCompany* magazine wrote in 2004. "[J. Jovan] Philyaw, the masterful pitchman behind the CueCat, a cutely named handheld barcode scanner that was supposed to bridge print media and the Web, apparently now does business under the name J. Hutton Pulitzer."[142]

Why is this important? Well, the citizens of Georgia should take note.

A Georgia Senate committee allowed Philyaw, who is also a failed treasure hunter, to speak for forty-eight minutes as "Jovan Hutton Pulitzer, inventor and pattern recognition expert," sharing his latest crackpot ideas on "kinematic artifact detection," which was unknown to the world before the Senate hearing.[143]

Philyaw–Pulitzer also claimed without evidence that he had "hacked" a poll pad. He further claimed that meant the entire voting system was compromised, even though the poll pad, like the poll books they have replaced, are never connected to the rest of the voting system.

Despite Pulitzer's claims, the poll pads are the only piece of election infrastructure ever connected to the internet, and they are never connected to the ballot-marking devices or scanners. The poll pads have a secure Wi-Fi capability that only responds to a single SSID so election workers can download updated voter lists to check people in on Election Day. But the Wi-Fi capability is disabled before the poll pads are put to use at the polling place.

Additionally, the touch screen interfaces and attached printers are never attached to the poll pads and are air-gapped so they cannot connect to the internet. Finally, the scanners used to tabulate the printed paper ballots, which voters can review before scanning, are not connected to any of the other equipment at any point either.

In a statement, poll pad creator KnowInk said:

> The assertions made about unauthorized access to our systems are patently false. The man claiming that someone "got into" our systems did not happen according to our forensic analysis. There was no "hack," there was no "back door" entry, there was no "pump and dump" and there was no access through a "thermostat" located hundreds of miles away in Savannah.[144]

Fake news is hard enough to combat when mainstream media outlets push it out, but when a small cadre of Georgia legislators turn the microphone to people like Philyaw–Pulitzer, it's a whole different story. This man is known for searching unsuccessfully for the Ark of the Covenant and later claiming that a sword, that was likely a fake, not only had "magical magnetic properties," but was also a sign that ancient Romans had visited North America by AD 200.[145]

These legislators needed to stop calling their own reelections illegitimate and focus on getting out the vote for the January 5 runoffs. The mistrust they were sowing was depressing turnout.

DECEMBER 31

TRUMP V. KEMP AND RAFFENSPERGER

On the last day of the year, long after Electoral College votes had been cast, President Trump sued Governor Kemp and me in Federal District Court, asking a judge to direct us to decertify Georgia's election results. The president relied on the same set of "facts" that had been rejected numerous times in courts already.

The attorney general's office went right to work on a response, even on New Year's Eve, so they could file on Monday. In the response, the attorney general wrote:

> There have been numerous suits filed since the November 3, 2020, general election, challenging most of the issues set forth in Plaintiff's [Trump's] motion. In all resolved suits, the claims have been flatly rejected. Plaintiff nevertheless seeks to disenfranchise millions of Georgia voters at the thirteenth hour—despite Plaintiff's own dilatory and confusing actions. Plaintiff lacks standing to bring the claims at issue, the Court should abstain from deciding this matter, and Plaintiff's claims are moot and otherwise frivolous.[146]

I left the office on Thursday afternoon looking forward to the long holiday weekend. Truth had prevailed in lawsuit after lawsuit since Election Day, and the certification of the Electoral College votes by Congress was now less than a week away. In 2021, I would begin work on my other priorities as secretary of state, streamlining and reforming licensing and regulations to make Georgia an even greater state to do business in.

CHAPTER 9

THE CALL

THIS BRINGS US BACK TO WHERE I BEGAN this book: President Donald Trump's phone call to me on January 2, 2021. The time was set, and Tricia and I sat on stools at our kitchen counter, waiting.

At 3:00 p.m. my cell phone rang. The area code was 202. Washington, D.C.

I answered, and Mark Meadows, the president's chief of staff, introduced himself.

What follows is a complete, unabridged transcript of the call, annotated with my thoughts at the time and further thoughts upon reflection.[147]

Mark Meadows: Okay. All right. Mr. President, everyone is on the line. This is Mark Meadows, the chief of staff. Just so we all are aware. On the line is secretary of state and two other individuals. Jordan [Fuchs, Georgia deputy secretary of state and chief of staff] and Mr. [Ryan] Germany [general counsel for the Georgia secretary of state's office] with him. You also have the attorneys that represent the president, Kurt [Hilbert] and Alex [Kaufman]; and Cleta Mitchell, who is not the attorney of record but has been involved; myself; and then the president. So, Mr. President, I'll turn it over to you.

President Trump: Okay, thank you very much. Hello, Brad and Ryan and everybody. We appreciate the time and the call. So we've spent a lot of time on this, and if we could just go over some of the numbers, I think it's pretty clear that we won. We won very substantially in Georgia. You even see it by rally size, frankly. We'd be getting 25- to 30,000 people a rally, and the competition would get less than 100 people. And it never made sense.

Observation: Yes, President Trump had large rallies with thousands of people. I attended one of those at the Macon airport that President Trump held for Governor Kemp when he was running for governor in 2018. They are exciting, play great music, and generate lots of energy. I watched many more rallies during the 2020 election cycle on cable news.

Not reported is that many of those people who attended the rallies came from other states. In the case of rallies held during Georgia's U.S. Senate runoff, many people attended but didn't live in Georgia and couldn't vote in our runoff. So the attendance in those cases gives a misleading impression of actual Georgia voters.

Also, as a candidate who has been in several political campaigns, I have found that elections are won with a comprehensive, multilayered campaign approach that includes yard signs, mailers, TV commercials, knocking on doors, and get-out-the-vote activities including phone banking, absentee ballot chase programs, and other activities. Successful campaigns are more than rallies.

President Trump: But we have a number of things. We have at least two or three—anywhere from 250- to 300,000 ballots were dropped mysteriously into the rolls. Much of that had to do with Fulton County, which hasn't been checked. We think that if you check the signatures—a real check of the signatures going back in Fulton County—you'll find at least a couple of hundred thousand of forged signatures of people who have been forged. And we are quite sure that's going to happen.

> *Observation: Fulton County had a total of 148,319 absentee votes in the November election, so mathematically it would be impossible to have 200,000 forged signatures on absentee ballots.*

President Trump: Another tremendous number. We're going to have an accurate number over the next two days with certified accountants. But an accurate number will be given, but it's in the 50s of thousands—and that's people that went to vote and they were told they can't vote because they've already been voted for. And it's a very sad thing. They walked out complaining. But the number's large. We'll have it for you. But it's much more than the number of 11,779 that's—the current margin is only 11,779. Brad, I think you agree with that, right? That's something I think everyone—at least that's a number that everyone agrees on.

> *Observation: The secretary of state's office never received a report from certified accountants for the Trump campaign. If thousands had been turned away from the polls as Trump describes, surely one of them would have contacted our office.*

President Trump: But that's the difference in the votes. But we've had hundreds of thousands of ballots that we're able to actually— We'll get you a pretty accurate number. You don't need much of a number because the number that in theory I lost by, the margin would be 11,779. But you also have a substantial numbers of people, thousands and thousands, who went to the voting place on

November 3, were told they couldn't vote, were told they couldn't vote because a ballot had been put in their name. And you know that's very, very, very, very sad.

Observation: There are no reports of thousands and thousands of voters being told they couldn't vote. If this had occurred, it would have made national news.

President Trump: We had, I believe it's about 4,502 voters who voted but who weren't on the voter registration list, so it's 4,502 who voted, but they weren't on the voter registration roll, which they had to be. You had 18,325 vacant address voters. The address was vacant, and they're not allowed to be counted. That's 18,325.

Observation: The first step in the voting process is to confirm the voter is registered to vote. A person who is not registered to vote cannot receive an absentee ballot and will not be allowed to vote at the poll. Evidence was never presented to back up the president's claim. Our office has a record of everyone who voted in Georgia (in fact, it's public record so everyone has it). All of them were registered to vote. Determining whether non-registered people voted is not difficult. Our investigation confirmed all voters were registered.

President Trump: Smaller number—you had 904 who only voted where they had just a P.O., a post office box number. And they had a post office box number, and that's not allowed.

Observation: A voter must register with a physical address. Of course, a voter's physical address may be different from the mailing address. Thousands of Georgians prefer to receive their mail, including an absentee ballot, at a post office mailbox. Also, many apartment and condominium developments have central locations for mail, and the addresses appear to be post office boxes.

While a few people do improperly register with P.O. boxes, coun-ties do their best to try to weed those out at the front end and get the voter's physical address. Our investigations have shown that a voter registered with a P.O. box generally lives in the district in which they voted.

President Trump: We had at least 18,000—that's on tape. We had them counted very painstakingly—18,000 voters having to do with [name redacted]. She's a vote scammer, a professional vote scammer and hustler. [Name redacted]. That was the tape that's been shown all over the world that makes everybody look bad. You, me, and everybody else.

Observation: I'm not including the name of the woman wrongly called a "scammer" and a "hustler." She deserves her privacy. President Trump's charge was not true. Every time you vote, you see people like her—older citizens who consider it their duty to serve our country in this way. They work a long day, or more, for very little money. Internet lies made this woman's life miserable.

President Trump: Where they got— Number one, they said very clearly, and it's been reported that they said there was a major water main break. Everybody fled the area. And then they came back, [name redacted] and her daughter and a few people. There were no Republican poll watchers. Actually, there were no Democrat poll watchers. I guess they were them. But there were no Democrats, either, and there was no law enforcement. Late in the morning, early in the morning, they went to the table with the black robe and the black shield, and they pulled out the votes. Those votes were put there a number of hours before. The table was put there. I think it was, Brad. You would know. It was probably eight hours or seven hours before, and then it was stuffed with votes.

> *Observation: This comment centers on the State Farm Arena disinformation campaign spread by Rudy Giuliani and his team. We addressed this rumor numerous times in November and December. State Farm Arena was under 24-7 video surveillance. There was no major water main break. One toilet in one bathroom was leaking. Nobody fled the area. At around 10:30 p.m., election workers at the arena were told they could go home for the night and come back on Wednesday morning to resume counting. Before leaving, they secured and sealed all of the ballots in boxes. Chris Harvey, the state elections director, told me, and I said they needed to keep counting. So he called, and they went back to work about forty minutes later. They reopened the boxes and removed the ballots. All of their movements are on video, reviewed by law enforcement and media. There were no extra ballots added.*

> *Giuliani and his team selectively sliced and diced the video and conjured up a false narrative to fit his disinformation campaign. The deliberate deceit worked. It convinced millions of people that [name redacted] had stolen the election.*

> *Granted, Fulton County has a long-standing history of election incompetence dating back to as far as 1994. I was the first secretary of state to get a consent agreement with Fulton County due to their election incompetence in the June 2020 primary that allowed us to put in an election monitor for the November election.*

President Trump: They weren't in an official voter box; they were in what looked to be suitcases or trunks. Suitcases. But they weren't in voter boxes.

Observation: They were in an official box for storing ballots, not trunks or suitcases. They were locked and sealed so they could not be tampered with.

President Trump: The minimum number it could be, because we watched it, and they watched it certified in slow motion instant replay if you can believe it, but slow motion, and it was magnified many times over. And the minimum it was 18,000 ballots, all for Biden.

Observation: These rumors spread by Rudy Giuliani and apparently believed by President Trump and his supporters have been thoroughly debunked by law enforcement, WSB-TV, and other news outlets. They watched the entire video and saw that ballots were not pulled out of boxes.

President Trump: You had out-of-state voters. They voted in Georgia, but they were from out of state, of 4,925. You had absentee ballots sent to vacant—, they were absentee ballots sent to vacant addresses. They had nothing on them about addresses, that's 2,326.

Observation: One illegal out-of-state voter is too many. These allegations were investigated using National Change of Address (NCOA) data from the U.S. Postal Service, voting data, and a questionnaire our investigators sent out to the approximately 8,000 potential out-of-state voters on the NCOA list. We found that almost every single voter the Trump campaign accused of being out of state was a legitimate Georgia voter who was only temporarily out of state for school, to take care of a relative, for work, or otherwise remained a Georgia resident. More people than usual were temporarily staying in their second homes in 2020 due to the COVID-19 pandemic. Based on that work, we estimate that fewer than 300 people statewide may have voted in Georgia after they moved out of state. That number is entirely too high for me and is why I prefer in-person voting with photo ID, but it's not close to changing the results of the election.

President Trump: And you had drop boxes, which is very bad. You had drop boxes that were picked up. We have photographs, and we have affidavits from many people. I don't know if you saw the hearings, but you have drop boxes where the box was picked up but not delivered for three days. So all sorts of things could have happened to that box, including, you know, putting in the votes that you wanted. So there were many infractions, and the bottom line is, many, many times the 11,779 margin that they said we lost by—we had vast, I mean the state is in turmoil over this.

Observation: Drop boxes were utilized in the November 2020 election because multiple reports in print and cable media highlighted the shortcomings of late and unreliable deliveries from the Postal Service. President Trump even echoed those concerns of post office incompetence, a federal agency for which he had oversight responsibility.

State regulations required drop boxes to be on government property, securely fastened to the ground, and under 24-7 surveillance. Ballots were collected daily and securely delivered to county election offices by two sworn county election officials who had to complete chain of custody documentation. The few instances of counties not properly completing that paperwork are under investigation. For example, one county election official who failed to keep appropriate documentation said she didn't think she had to because the only drop box was right outside her office and she emptied it herself every day. She should have done the paperwork, but that's not evidence of fraud or ballot harvesting. Boxes were locked tight at 7:00 p.m. election night so no late-arriving ballots could be accepted.

President Trump: And I know you would like to get to the bottom of it, although I saw you on television today, and you said that you found nothing wrong. I mean, you know, and I didn't lose the state, Brad. People have been saying that it was the highest vote ever. There was no way. A lot of the political people said that there's no way they beat me. And they beat me. They beat me in the— As you know, every single state, we won every state. We won every statehouse in the country. We held the Senate, which is shocking to people, although we'll see what happens tomorrow or in a few days.

Observation: Republican presidential candidates have not carried the Northeast or the West Coast for over twenty-five years. Republicans did not carry every statehouse in the country. Republicans had good results, and Republicans currently hold the legislatures in about thirty states, but not all fifty.

President Trump: The other thing, dead people. So dead people voted, and I think the number is close to 5,000 people. And they went to obituaries. They went to all sorts of methods to come up with an accurate number, and a minimum is close to about 5,000 voters.

Observation: The actual number is two, not 5,000. While one is too many, we have identified two votes from beyond the grave, and they are both situations where family members voted for the recently deceased person. Unacceptable, but not widespread fraud and not different than what has been seen in past elections. The perpetrators will be brought in front of the State Election Board.

President Trump: The bottom line is, when you add it all up and then you start adding, you know, 300,000 fake ballots.

Observation: Presumably he's talking about the absentee ballots that were counted early Wednesday morning. They were neither fake nor unexpected.

President Trump: Then the other thing they said is in Fulton County and other areas. And this may or may not be true ... this just came up this morning, that they are burning their ballots, that they are shredding, shredding ballots and removing equipment. They're changing the equipment on the Dominion machines and, you know, that's not legal.

Observation: There was no burning of anything and no shredding of ballots. Absentee ballot blank envelopes in Cobb County were shredded after the ballots were removed. None of the equipment was changed.

President Trump: And they supposedly shredded, I think they said 300 pounds of, 3,000 pounds of ballots. And that just came to us as a report today. And it is a very sad situation.

Observation: Again, no ballots were shredded.

President Trump: But Brad, if you took the minimum numbers where many, many times above the 11,779, and many of those numbers are certified, or they will be certified, but they are certified. And those are numbers that are there, that exist. And that beat the margin of loss, they beat it, I mean, by a lot, and people should be happy to have an accurate count instead of an election where there's turmoil.

I mean there's turmoil in Georgia and other places. You're not the only one, I mean. We have other states that I believe will be flipping to us very shortly. And this is something that— you know, as an example, I think it in Detroit, I think there's a section, a good section of your state actually, which we're not sure so we're not going to report it yet. But in Detroit, we had, I think it was, 139 percent of the people voted. That's not too good.

In Pennsylvania, they had well over 200,000 more votes than they had people voting. And that doesn't play too well, and the legislature there is, which is Republican, is extremely activist and angry. I mean, there were other things also that were almost as bad as that. But they had as an example, in Michigan, a tremendous number of dead people that voted. I think it was, I think, Mark, it was 18,000. Some unbelievably high number, much higher than yours, you were in the 4- to 5,000 category.

And that was checked out laboriously by going through, by going through the obituary columns in the newspapers.

So I guess, with all of it being said, Brad, the bottom line, and provisional ballots, again, you know, you'll have to tell me about the provisional ballots, but we have a lot of people that were complaining that they weren't able to vote because they were already voted for. These are great people.

And, you know, they were shell-shocked. I don't know if you call that provisional ballots. In some states, we had a lot of provisional ballot situations where people were given a provisional ballot because when they walked in on November 3 and they were already voted for.

So that's it. I mean, we have many, many times the number of votes necessary to win the state. And we won the state, and we won it very substantially and easily, and we're getting, we have, much of this is a very certified, far more certified than we need. But we're getting additional numbers certified, too. And we're getting pictures of drop boxes being delivered and delivered late. Delivered three days later, in some cases, plus we have many affidavits to that effect.

Mark Meadows: So, Mr. President, if I might be able to jump in, and I'll give Brad a chance. Mr. Secretary, obviously there is, there are allegations where we believe that not every vote or fair vote and legal vote was counted, and that's at odds with the representation from the secretary of state's office.

What I'm hopeful for is there some way that we can, we can find some kind of agreement to look at this a little bit more fully? You know the president mentioned Fulton County.

But in some of these areas where there seems to be a difference of where the facts seem to lead, and so Mr. Secretary, I was hopeful that, you know, in the spirit of cooperation and compromise, is there something that we can at least have a discussion to look at some of these allegations to find a path forward that's less litigious?

Brad Raffensperger: Well, I listened to what the president has just said. President Trump, we've had several lawsuits, and we've had to respond in court to the lawsuits and the contentions. We don't agree that you have won.

> *Observation: President Trump had just talked for almost twenty minutes, claiming that he had won the election. He had also filed a lawsuit against us the previous week. These were my first words on the call, and I needed to say, from the outset, that I disagreed with him. I could not give his lawyer the opportunity in a deposition or in court to say to me, "You never disputed what he said." I had to be very clear and precise that the facts did not support his statements.*

Brad Raffensperger: And we don't, I didn't agree about the 200,000 number that you'd mentioned. I'll go through that point by point. What we have done is we gave our state Senate about one and a half hours of our time going through the election issue by issue and then on the state House, the Government

Affairs Committee, we gave them about two and a half hours of our time, going back point by point on all the issues of contention. And then just a few days ago, we met with our U.S. congressmen, Republican congressmen, and we gave them about two hours of our time talking about this past election.

> *Observation: During the ongoing Trump disinformation campaign, our office provided detailed fact-based information debunking every piece of misinformation and disinformation generated by President Trump's supporters during hearings with the Georgia State Senate committee and State House committee, plus a phone conversation with the Republican members of the U.S. House of Representatives Government Oversight Committee.*

Brad Raffensperger: Going back, primarily what you've talked about here focused in on primarily, I believe, is the absentee ballot process. I don't believe that you're really questioning the Dominion machines. Because we did a hand retally, a 100 percent retally of all the ballots, and compared them to what the machines said and came up with virtually the same result. Then we did the recount, and we got virtually the same result. So I guess we can probably take that off the table. I don't think there's an issue about that.

President Trump: Well, Brad, not that there's not an issue, because we have a big issue with Dominion in other states and perhaps in yours. But we haven't felt we needed to go there. And just to, you know, maybe put a little different spin on what Mark is saying, Mark Meadows, yeah, we'd like to go further, but we don't really need to. We have all the votes we need.

You know, we won the state. If you took, these are the most minimal numbers, the numbers that I gave you, those are numbers that are certified, your absentee ballots sent to vacant addresses, your out-of-state voters, 4,925. You know when you add them up, it's many more times, it's many times the 11,779 number. So we could go through, we have not gone through your Dominion. So we can't give them blessing. I mean, in other states, we think we found tremendous corruption with Dominion machines, but we'll have to see.

But we only lost the state by that number, 11,000 votes—and 779. So with that being said, with just what we have, with just what we have, we're giving you minimal, minimal numbers. We're doing the most conservative numbers possible. We're many times, many, many times above the margin. And so we don't really have to, Mark, I don't think we have to go through—

Mark Meadows: Right.

President Trump: Because what's the difference between winning the election by two votes and winning it by half a million votes? I think I probably did win it by half a million. You know, one of the things that happened, Brad, is we have other people coming in now from Alabama and from South Carolina and from other states, and they're saying it's impossible for you to have lost Georgia. We won. You know, in Alabama, we set a record, got the highest vote ever. In Georgia, we set a record with a massive amount of votes. And they say it's not possible to have lost Georgia.

And I could tell you by our rallies. I could tell you by the rally I'm having on Monday night, the place, they already have lines of people standing out front waiting. It's just not possible to have lost Georgia. It's not possible. When I heard it was close, I said there's no way. But they dropped a lot of votes in there late at night. You know that, Brad. And that's what we are working on very, very stringently. But regardless of those votes, with all of it being said, we lost by essentially 11,000 votes, and we have many more votes already calculated and certified, too.

And so I just don't know, you know, Mark, I don't know what's the purpose. I won't give Dominion a pass because we found too many bad things. But we don't need Dominion or anything else.

We have won this election in Georgia based on all of this. And there's nothing wrong with saying that, Brad. You know, I mean, having the correct— The people of Georgia are angry. And these numbers are going to be repeated on Monday night. Along with others that we're going to have by that time, which are much more substantial even. And the people of Georgia are angry, the people of the country are angry. And there's nothing wrong with saying that, you know, that you've recalculated. Because the 2,236 in absentee ballots. I mean, they're all exact numbers that were done by accounting firms, law firms, etc. And even if you cut 'em in half, cut 'em in half and cut 'em in half again, it's more votes than we need.

> *Observation: Oh, I understand better than anyone else that people are angry. Due to the disinformation and misinformation fed to the people from President Trump and his team and since Georgia has been a reliably red state since 2000, voters didn't understand how he lost. Factor in the president's rhetoric that I was an "enemy of the state" and the bull's-eye put on my back on the enemy of the state website, along with more than twenty other election officials—Georgians and the nation were lathered into a tizzy.*
>
> *But the facts are the facts, and our facts are correct. Therefore, for the office of the secretary of state to "recalculate" would mean we would somehow have to fudge the numbers. The president*

was asking me to do something that I knew was wrong, and I was not going to do that.

Brad Raffensperger: Well, Mr. President, the challenge that you have is the data you have is wrong. We talked to the congressmen, and they were surprised.

Observation: Yes, many of the congressman said they were surprised during my call with them to explain that Georgia's counties were still doing signature match. Due to the huge disinformation campaign waged by Trump surrogates, the congressmen and the general populace believed this practice of signature match had been stopped. Nothing could be further from the truth. Signature match is required by state law and was not weakened or stopped. In fact, we actually strengthened it in 2020 and even made GBI signature-match identification training available for county election officials.

Brad Raffensperger: But they, I guess there was a person named Mr. Braynard who came to these meetings and presented data, and he said that there were dead people, I believe it was upward of 5,000. The actual number were two. Two. Two people that were dead that voted. So that's wrong.

President Trump: Well, Cleta, how do you respond to that? Maybe you tell me?

Cleta Mitchell: Well, I would say, Mr. Secretary, one of the things that we have requested and what we said was, if you look, if you read our petition, it said that we took the names and birth years, and we had certain information available to us. We have asked from your office for records that only you have, and so we said there is a universe of people who have the same name and same birth year and died.

But we don't have the records that you have. And one of the things that we have been suggesting formally and informally for weeks now is for you to make available to us the records that would be necessary—

Observation: Cleta Mitchell was asking for certain personal information on voters. Georgia law requires that we protect that information and not share it with political campaigns.

President Trump: But, Cleta, even before you do that, and not even including that, that's why I hardly even included that number. Although in one state, we have a tremendous amount of dead people. So I don't know. I'm sure we do in Georgia, too. I'm sure we do in Georgia, too.

But we're so far ahead. We're so far ahead of these numbers, even the phony ballots of [name redacted], known scammer. You know the internet? You know what was trending on the internet? "Where's [name redacted]?" Because they thought she'd be in jail. "Where's [name redacted]?" It's crazy, it's crazy. That was. The minimum number is 18,000 for [name redacted], but they think it's probably about 56,000, but the minimum number is 18,000 on the [name redacted] night where she ran back in there when everybody was gone and stuffed, she stuffed the ballot boxes.

Let's face it, Brad, I mean. They did it in slow motion replay, magnified, right? She stuffed the ballot boxes. They were stuffed like nobody has ever seen them stuffed before.

So there's a term for it when it's a machine instead of a ballot box, but she stuffed the machine. She stuffed the ballot. Each ballot went three times, they were showing: Here's ballot number 1. Here it is a second time, third time, next ballot.

I mean, look. Brad. We have a new tape that we're going to release. It's devastating. And by the way, that one event, that one event is much more than the 11,000 votes that we're talking about. It's, you know, that one event was a disaster. And it's just, you know. But it was, it was something. It can't be disputed. And again, we have a version that you haven't seen, but it's magnified. It's magnified, and you can see everything. For some reason, they put it in three times, each ballot, and I don't know why. I don't know why three times. Why not five times, right? Go ahead.

Brad Raffensperger: You're talking about the State Farm video. And I think it's extremely unfortunate that Rudy Giuliani or his people, they sliced and diced that video and took it out of context. The next day, we brought in WSB-TV, and we let them show, see the full run of tape, and what you'll see, the events that transpired are nowhere near what was projected by, you know —

President Trump: But where were the poll watchers, Brad? There were no poll watchers there. There were no Democrats or Republicans. There was no security there.

It was late in the evening, late in the—, early in the morning, and there was nobody else in the room. Where were the poll watchers. And why did they say a water main broke? Which they did and which was reported in the newspapers. They said they left. They ran out because of a water main break, and there was no water main. There was nothing. There was no break. There was no water main break. But we're, if you take out everything, where were the Republican poll watchers? Even where were the Democrat poll watchers? Because there were none.

And then you say, well, they left their station. You know, if you look at the tape, and this was, this was reviewed by professional police and detectives and other people. When they left in a rush, everybody left in a rush because of the water main. But everybody left in a rush. These people left their station.

When they came back, they didn't go to their station. They went to the apron, wrapped around the table, under which were thousands and thousands of ballots in a box that was not an official or a sealed box. And then they took those. They went back to a different station. So if they would have come back, they would have walked to their station, and they would have continued to work. But they couldn't do even that, because that's illegal. Because they had no Republican poll watchers. And remember, her reputation is — she's known all over the internet, Brad. She's known all over.

I'm telling you, "Where's [name redacted]" was one of the hot items ... [Name redacted.] They knew her. "Where's [name redacted]?" So, Brad, there can be no justification for that. And I, you know, I give everybody the benefit of the doubt. But that was— And, Brad, why did they put the votes in three times? You know, they put 'em in three times.

Brad Raffensperger: Mr. President, they did not put that. We did an audit of that, and we proved conclusively that they were not scanned three times.

President Trump: Where was everybody else at that late time in the morning? Where was everybody? Where were the Republicans? Where were the security guards? Where were the people that were there just a little while before when everyone ran out of the room? How come we had no security in the room? Why did they run to the bottom of the table? Why do they run there and just open the skirt and rip out the votes? I mean, Brad. And they were sitting there, I think for five hours or something like that, the votes.

Brad Raffensperger: Mr. President, we'll send you the link from WSB.

President Trump: I don't care about the link. I don't need it. Brad, I have a much better—

Cleta Mitchell: I will tell you. I've seen the tape. The full tape. So has Alex. We've watched it. And what we saw and what we've confirmed in the timing is that they made everybody leave. We have sworn affidavits saying that. And then they began to process ballots. And our estimate is that there were roughly 18,000 ballots. We don't know that. If you know that—

President Trump: It was 18,000 ballots, but they used each one three times.

Cleta Mitchell: Well, I don't know about that, but I know —

President Trump: Well, I do, because we had ours magnified out —

Cleta Mitchell: I've watched the entire tape.

President Trump: But nobody can make a case for that, Brad. Nobody. I mean, look, that's, you'd have to be a child to think anything other than that. Just a child. I mean you have your never-Trumper U.S. attorney there—

> *Observation: President Trump is referring to Byung Jin "BJay" Pak, U.S. attorney for the Northern District of Georgia. President Trump nominated Pak for the post in 2017, and Pak was praised at the time by Georgia's U.S. senators, Johnny Isakson and David Perdue. He is a person of high character and decency, and his office and the FBI had open access to our investigative processes and witness interviews.*

Cleta Mitchell: How many ballots, Mr. Secretary, are you saying were processed then?

Brad Raffensperger: We had GBI … investigate that.

Ryan Germany: We had our— This is Ryan Germany. We had our law enforcement officers talk to everyone who was, who was there after that event came to light. GBI was with them as well as FBI agents.

President Trump: Well, there's no way they could— Then they're incompetent. They're either dishonest or incompetent, okay?

> *Observation: The Georgia office of secretary of state has twenty-two post-certified law enforcement officers. They are sworn to uphold every law in Georgia. There has never been a hint of scandal from this office under my watch, or any of the previous secretaries of state. In addition, our office requested from Governor Kemp and received additional law enforcement resources from the Georgia Bureau of Investigation. Both of these organizations are run with integrity, and their character is not to be impugned. The FBI is our nation's top law enforcement agency.*

Cleta Mitchell: Well, what did they find?

President Trump: There's only two answers, dishonesty or incompetence. There's just no way. Look. There's no way. And on the other thing, I said too, there is no way. I mean, there's no way that these things could have been, you know, you have all these different people that voted, but they don't live in Georgia anymore. What was that number, Cleta? That was a pretty good number, too.

Cleta Mitchell: The number who have registered out of state after they moved from Georgia. And so they had a date when they moved from Georgia, they registered to vote out of state, and then it's like 4,500. I don't have that number right in front of me.

President Trump: And then they came back in, and they voted.

Cleta Mitchell: And voted. Yeah.

President Trump: I thought that was a large number, though. It was in the 20s.

Ryan Germany: We've been going through each of those as well, and those numbers that we got, that Ms. Mitchell was just saying, they're not accurate. Every one we've been through are people that lived in Georgia, moved to a different state, but then moved back to Georgia legitimately. And in many cases—

President Trump: How many people do that? They moved out, and then they said, "Ah, to hell with it, I'll move back." You know, it doesn't sound like a very normal ... You mean, they moved out, and what, they missed it so much that they wanted to move back in? It's crazy.

Ryan Germany: They moved back in years ago. This was not like something just before the election. So there's something about that data that, it's just not accurate.

President Trump: Well, I don't know. All I know is that it is certified. And they moved out of Georgia, and they voted. It didn't say they moved back in, Cleta, did it?

Cleta Mitchell: No, but I mean, we're looking at the voter registration. Again, if you have additional records, we've been asking for that, but you haven't shared any of that with us. You just keep saying you investigated the allegations.

President Trump: Cleta, a lot of it you don't need to be shared. I mean, to be honest, they should share it. They should share it because you want to get to an honest election.

I won this election by hundreds of thousands of votes. There's no way I lost Georgia. There's no way. We won by hundreds of thousands of votes. I'm just going by small numbers, when you add them up, they're many times the 11,000. But I won that state by hundreds of thousands of votes.

Do you think it's possible that they shredded ballots in Fulton County? Because that's what the rumor is. And also that Dominion took out machines. That Dominion is really moving fast to get rid of their, uh, machinery.

Do you know anything about that? Because that's illegal, right?

Ryan Germany: This is Ryan Germany. No, Dominion has not moved any machinery out of Fulton County.

President Trump: But have they moved the inner parts of the machines and replaced them with other parts?

Ryan Germany: No.

President Trump: Are you sure, Ryan?

Ryan Germany: I'm sure. I'm sure, Mr. President.

President Trump: What about, what about the ballots. The shredding of the ballots. Have they been shredding ballots?

Ryan Germany: The only investigation that we have into that— they have not been shredding any ballots. There was an issue in Cobb County where they were doing normal office shredding, getting rid of old stuff, and we investigated that. But this stuff from, you know, from, you know, past elections.

President Trump: It doesn't pass the smell test because we hear they're shredding thousands and thousands of ballots. And now what they're saying, "Oh, we're just cleaning up the office." You know.

Brad Raffensperger: Mr. President, the problem you have with social media, they—People can say anything.

President Trump: Oh, this isn't social media. This is Trump media. It's not social media. It's really not. It's not social media. I don't care about social media. I couldn't care less. Social media is Big Tech. Big Tech is on your side, you know. I don't even know why you have a side because you should want to have an accurate election. And you're a Republican.

Brad Raffensperger: We believe that we do have an accurate election.

President Trump: No, no you don't. No, no you don't. You don't have. Not even close. You're off by hundreds of thousands of votes. And just on the small numbers, you're off on these numbers, and these numbers can't be just— Well, why won't?— Okay. So you sent us into Cobb County for signature verification, right? You sent us into Cobb County, which we didn't want to go into. And you said it would be open to the public. So we had our experts there. They weren't allowed into the room. But we didn't want Cobb County. We wanted Fulton County. And you wouldn't give it to us. Now, why aren't we doing signature— And why can't it be open to the public?

And why can't we have professionals do it instead of rank amateurs who will never find anything and don't want to find anything? They don't want to find, you know, they don't want to find anything. Someday you'll tell me the reason why, because I don't understand your reasoning. But someday you'll tell me the reason why. But why don't you want to find?

Ryan Germany: Mr. President, we chose Cobb County —

President Trump: Why don't you want to find— What?

Ryan Germany: Sorry, go ahead.

President Trump: So why did you do Cobb County? We didn't even request— We requested Fulton County, not Cobb County. Go ahead, please. Go ahead.

Ryan Germany: We chose Cobb County because that was the only county where there's been any evidence submitted that the signature verification was not properly done.

President Trump: No, but I told you. We're not, we're not saying that.

Cleta Mitchell: We did say that.

President Trump: Fulton County. Look. Stacey [Abrams], in my opinion, Stacey is as dishonest as they come. She has outplayed you ... at everything. She got you to sign a totally unconstitutional agreement, which is a disastrous agreement. You can't check signatures.

> *Observation: President Trump is wrong on this issue. The settlement agreement required that county election officials confirm signatures and reject any ballots where they determined the signature did not match.*

President Trump: I can't imagine you're allowed to do harvesting, I guess, in that agreement. That agreement is a disaster for this country. But she got you somehow to sign that thing, and she has outsmarted you at every step.

And I hate to imagine what's going to happen on Monday or Tuesday, but it's very scary to people. You know, when the ballots flow in out of nowhere. It's very scary to people. That consent decree is a disaster. It's a disaster. A very good lawyer who examined it said they've never seen anything like it.

Brad Raffensperger: Harvesting is still illegal in the state of Georgia. And that settlement agreement did not change that one iota.

> *Observation: One of my first actions upon taking office in 2019 was to outlaw ballot harvesting with the passage of HB 319, which was signed into law.*

President Trump: It's not a settlement agreement, it's a consent decree. It even says consent decree on it, doesn't it? It uses the term consent decree. It doesn't say settlement agreement. It's a consent decree. It's a disaster.

Brad Raffensperger: It's a settlement agreement.

President Trump: What's written on top of it?

Brad Raffensperger: Ryan?

Ryan Germany: I don't have it in front of me, but it was not entered by the court, it's not a court order.

President Trump: But Ryan, it's called a consent decree, is that right? On the paper. Is that right?

Ryan Germany: I don't believe so, but I don't have it in front of me.

> *Observation: The official name of the document is "Compromise Settlement Agreement and Release," signed by Georgia Attorney General Chris Carr and special outside counsel Attorney Vincent Russo.*
>
> *As I mentioned earlier, Vincent Russo has been the general counsel for the Georgia Republican Party.*
>
> *The settlement agreement did not eliminate signature matching. To the contrary, it ensured that signature matching remained in effect and that non-matching signatures be rejected in the face of a challenge to that state law. Signature matching was performed twice: at the absentee ballot application phase and when the signed absentee ballot, with its envelope with the voter's signature, was returned to the election office.*
>
> *After losing Georgia and as part of the blame shifting, this document has been misnamed as a consent decree and mischaracterized to do something it had no power to do.*

President Trump: Okay, whatever. It's a disaster. It's a disaster. Look. Here's the problem. We can go through signature verification, and we'll find hundreds of thousands of signatures, if you let us do it. And the only way you can do it, as you know, is to go to the past.

But you didn't do that in Cobb County. You just looked at one page compared to another. The only way you can do a signature verification is go from the one that signed it on November whatever. Recently. And compare it to two years ago, four years ago, six years ago, you know, or even one. And you'll find that you have many different signatures. But in Fulton, where they dumped ballots, you will find that you have many that aren't even signed and you have many that are forgeries.

Okay, you know that. You know that. You have no doubt about that. And you will find you will be at 11,779 within minutes because Fulton County is totally corrupt, and so is she totally corrupt.

And they're going around playing you and laughing at you behind your back, Brad, whether you know it or not. They're laughing at you. And you've taken a state that's a Republican state, and you've made it almost impossible for a Republican to win because of cheating, because they cheated like nobody's ever cheated before. And I don't care how long it takes me, you know, we're going to have other states coming forward—pretty good.

Observation: President Trump is now turning to ridicule, perhaps thinking a shot at my ego will persuade me to do something that I knew wasn't right and had no power to do.

President Trump: But I won't … this is never … this is … We have some incredible talent said they've never seen anything … Now the problem is they need more time for the big numbers. But they're very substantial numbers. But I think you're going to find that they— By the way, a little information— I think you're going to find that they are shredding ballots because they have to get rid of the ballots because the ballots are unsigned. The ballots are corrupt, and they're brand new, and they don't have seals, and there's a whole thing with the ballots. But the ballots are corrupt.

And you are going to find that they are— Which is totally illegal— It is more illegal for you than it is for them, because, you know what they did and you're not reporting it. That's a criminal, that's a criminal offense. And you can't let that happen. That's a big risk to you and to Ryan, your lawyer. And that's a big risk.

> *Observation: Now President Trump is using what he believes is the power of his position to threaten Ryan and me with prosecution if we don't do what he tells us to do. It was nothing but an attempt at manipulation.*

President Trump: But they are shredding ballots, in my opinion, based on what I've heard. And they are removing machinery, and they're moving it as fast as they can. Both of which are criminal fines. And you can't let it happen, and you are letting it happen. You know, I mean, I'm notifying you that you're letting it happen.

> *Observation: Again, no ballots were shredded, and voting machines were secured and stored. Every piece of voting equipment.*

President Trump: So look. All I want to do is this. I just want to find 11,780 votes, which is one more than we have, because we won the state.

> *Observation: The president now is directly telling us what he wants—the exact number of votes he needs to win Georgia.*

President Trump: And flipping the state is a great testament to our country because, you know, this is . . . it's a testament that they can admit to a mistake or whatever you want to call it. If it was a mistake, I don't know. A lot of people think it wasn't a mistake. It was much more criminal than that. But it's a big problem in Georgia, and it's not a problem that's going away. I mean, you know, it's not a problem that's going away.

Ryan Germany: This is Ryan. We're looking into every one of those things that you mentioned.

President Trump: Good. But if you find it, you've got to say it, Ryan.

Ryan Germany: Let me tell you what we are seeing. What we're seeing is not at all what you're describing. These are investigators from our office, these are investigators from GBI, and they're looking, and they're good. And that's not what they're seeing. And we'll keep looking at all these things.

President Trump: Well, you better check on the ballots because they are shredding ballots, Ryan. I'm just telling you, Ryan. They're shredding ballots. And you should look at that very carefully. Because that's so illegal. You know, you may not even believe it because it's so bad. But they're shredding ballots because they think we're going to eventually get there ... Because we'll eventually get into Fulton. In my opinion, it's never too late. ... So, that's the story. Look, we need only 11,000 votes. We have far more than that as it stands now. We'll have more and more. And ... do you have provisional ballots at all, Brad? Provisional ballots?

Brad Raffensperger: Provisional ballots are allowed by state law.

President Trump: Sure, but I mean, are they counted, or did you just hold them back, because they, you know, in other words, how many provisional ballots do you have in the state?

Brad Raffensperger: We'll get you that number.

President Trump: Because most of them are made out to the name Trump. Because these are people that were scammed when they came in. And we have thousands of people that have testified or that want to testify. When they came in, they were proudly going to vote on November 3. And they were told, "I'm sorry, you've already been voted for, you've already voted." The women, men started screaming, "No. I proudly voted till November 3." They said, "I'm sorry, but you've already been voted for, and you have a ballot." And these people are beside themselves. So they went out, and they filled in a provisional ballot, putting the name Trump on it.

And what about that batch of military ballots that came in? And even though I won the military by a lot, it was 100 percent Trump. I mean 100 percent Biden. Do you know about that? A large group of ballots came in, I think it was to Fulton County, and they just happened to be 100 percent for Trump— for Biden—even though Trump won the military by a lot, you know, a tremendous amount. But these ballots were 100 percent for Biden. And do you know about that? A very substantial number came in, all for Biden. Does anybody know about it?

Cleta Mitchell: I know about it, but—

President Trump: Okay, Cleta, I'm not asking you, Cleta, honestly. I'm asking Brad. Do you know about the military ballots that we have confirmed now? Do you know about the military ballots that came in that were 100 percent, I mean 100 percent, for Biden. Do you know about that?

Ryan Germany: I don't know about that. I do know that we have, when military ballots come in, it's not just military, it's also military and overseas citizens. The military part of that does generally go Republican. The overseas citizen part of it generally goes very Democrat. This was a mix of them.

President Trump: No, but this was. That's okay. But I got like 78 percent of the military. These ballots were all for … They didn't tell me overseas. Could be overseas too, but I get votes overseas, too, Ryan, in all fairness. No they came in, a large batch came in, and it was, quote, 100 percent for Biden. And that is criminal. You know, that's criminal. Okay. That's another criminal, that's another of the many criminal events, many criminal events here.

I don't know. Look, Brad. I got to get … I have to find 12,000 votes, and I have them times a lot. And therefore I won the state. That's before we go to the next step, which is in the process of right now. You know, and I watched you this morning, and you said, well, there was no criminality.

But I mean all of this stuff is very dangerous stuff. When you talk about no criminality, I think it's very dangerous for you to say that.

Observation: I felt then—and still believe today—that this was a threat. Others obviously thought so, too, because some of Trump's more radical followers have responded as if it was their duty to carry out this threat.

President Trump: I just, I just don't know why you don't want to have the votes counted as they are. Like even you when you went and did that check. And I was surprised because, you know … And we found a few thousand votes that were against me. I was actually surprised because the way that check was done, all you're doing, you know, recertifying existing votes and, you know, and you were given votes and you just counted them up, and you still found 3,000 that were bad. So that was sort of surprising that it came down to three or five, I don't know. Still a lot of votes. But you have to go back to check from past years with respect to signatures. And if you check with Fulton County, you'll have hundreds of thousands, because they dumped ballots into Fulton County and the other county next to it.

Observation: Again, we counted the votes three times. We counted every paper ballot by hand. Law enforcement officers investigated the charges made by President Trump and his campaign, and they were all empty charges.

President Trump: So, what are we going to do here, folks? I only need 11,000 votes. Fellas, I need 11,000 votes. Give me a break.

Observation: This repeated request for votes showed me that President Trump really had no idea how elections work. The secretary of state's office doesn't allocate any votes.

President Trump: You know, we have that in spades already. Or we can keep it going, but that's not fair to the voters of Georgia because they're going to see what happened, and they're going to see what happened. I mean, I'll, I'll take on anybody you want with regard to [name redacted] and her lovely daughter, a very lovely young lady, I'm sure. But, but [name redacted] ... I will take on anybody you want. And the minimum, there were 18,000 ballots, but they used them three times. So that's, you know, a lot of votes. And they were all to Biden, by the way, that's the other thing we didn't say. You know, [name redacted], the one thing I forgot to say, which was the most important. You know that every single ballot she did went to Biden. You know that, right? Do you know that, by the way, Brad?

Every single ballot that she did through the machines at early, early in the morning went to Biden. Did you know that, Ryan?

Ryan Germany: That's not accurate, Mr. President.

President Trump: Huh? What is accurate?

Ryan Germany: The numbers that we are showing are accurate.

President Trump: No, about [name redacted]. About early in the morning, Ryan. Where the woman took, you know, when the whole gang took the stuff from under the table, right? Do you know, do you know who those ballots, do you know who they were made out to? Do you know who they were voting for?

Ryan Germany: No, not specifically.

President Trump: Did you ever check?

Ryan Germany: We did what I described to you earlier—

President Trump: No. No. No. Did you ever check the ballots that were scanned by [name redacted], a known political operative, balloteer? Did you ever check who those votes were for?

Ryan Germany: We looked into that situation that you described.

President Trump: No, they were 100 percent for Biden. One hundred percent. There wasn't a Trump vote in the whole group. Why don't you want to find this, Ryan? What's wrong with you? I heard your lawyer is very difficult, actually. But I'm sure you're a good lawyer. You have a nice last name.

But, but I'm just curious, why wouldn't, why do you keep fighting this thing? It just doesn't make sense. We're way over the 17,779, right? We're way over that number, and just if you took just [name redacted]. We're over that number by five, five or six times when you multiply that times three. And every single ballot went to Biden, and you didn't know that. But now you know it.

So tell me, Brad, what are we going to do? We won the election, and it's not fair to take it away from us like this. And it's going to be very costly in many ways. And I think you have to say that you're going to reexamine it, and you can reexamine it, but reexamine it with people that want to find answers, not people that don't want to find answers.

Observation: We recounted, we reexamined with professional law enforcement officers, and we found the answers. They were not the answers President Trump wanted to hear, but they were the facts—true and correct answers.

President Trump: For instance, I'm hearing Ryan that he's probably, I'm sure a great lawyer and everything, but he's making statements about those ballots that he doesn't know. But he's making them with such— He did make them with surety. But now I think he's less sure because the answer is, they all went to Biden, and that alone wins us the election by a lot. You know, so.

Brad Raffensperger: Mr. President, you have people that submit information, and we have our people that submit information. And then it comes before the court, and the court then has to make a determination. We have to stand by our numbers. We believe our numbers are right.

President Trump: Why do you say that, though? I don't know. I mean, sure, we can play this game with the courts, but why do you say that? First of all, they don't even assign us a judge. They don't even assign us a judge. But why wouldn't you ... Hey Brad, why wouldn't you want to check out [name redacted]? And why wouldn't you want to say, hey, if, in fact, President Trump is right about that, then he wins the state of Georgia. Just that one incident alone without going through hundreds of thousands of dropped ballots. You just say, you stick by, I mean I've been watching you, you know. You don't care about anything. "Your numbers are right." But your numbers aren't right. They're really wrong, and they're really wrong, Brad. And I know this phone call is going nowhere other than, other than ultimately, you know— Look, ultimately, I win, okay? Because you guys are so wrong. And you treated this . . . You treated the population of Georgia so badly. You, between you and your governor, who is down at twenty-one, he was down twenty-one points. And like a schmuck, I endorsed him, and he got elected. But I will tell you, he is a disaster.

The people are so angry in Georgia, I can't imagine he's ever getting elected again, I'll tell you that much right now. But why wouldn't you want to find the right answer, Brad, instead of keep saying that the numbers are right? Because those numbers are so wrong.

Cleta Mitchell: Mr. Secretary, Mr. President, one of the things that we have been, Alex can talk about this, we talked about it, and I don't know whether the information has been conveyed to your office, but I think what the president is saying, and what we've been trying to do is to say, look, the court is not acting on our petition. They haven't even assigned a judge. But the people of Georgia and the people of America have a right to know the answers. And you have data and records that we don't have access to.

And you can keep telling us and making public statements that you investigated this and nothing to see here. But we don't know about that. All we know is what you tell us. What I don't understand is why wouldn't it be in everyone's best interest to try to get to the bottom, compare the numbers, you know, if you say, because ... to try to be able to get to the truth because we don't have any way of confirming what you're telling us. You tell us that you had an investigation at the State Farm Arena. I don't have any report. I've never seen a report of investigation. I don't know that is. I've been pretty involved in this, and I don't know. And that's just one of twenty-five categories. And it doesn't even. And as I, as the president said, we haven't even gotten into the Dominion issue. That's not part of our case. It's not part of, we just didn't feel as though we had any to be able to develop—

President Trump: No, we do have a way, but I don't want to get into it. We found a way ... Excuse me, but we don't need it because we're only down 11,000 votes. So we don't even need it. I personally think they're corrupt as hell. But we don't need that. All we have to do, Cleta, is find 11,000-plus votes. So we don't need that. I'm not looking to shake up the whole world. We won Georgia easily. We won it by hundreds of thousands of votes. But if you go by basic, simple numbers, we won it easily, easily. So we're not giving Dominion a pass on the record. We don't need Dominion because we have so many other votes that we don't need to prove it any more than we already have.

Kurt Hilbert: Mr. President and Cleta, this is Kurt Hilbert, if I might interject for a moment. Ryan, I would like to suggest that just four categories that have already been mentioned by the president that have actually hard numbers of 24,149 votes that were counted illegally. That in and of itself is sufficient to change the results or place the outcome in doubt. We would like to sit down with your office, and we can do it through purposes of compromise and just like this phone call, just to deal with that limited category of votes. And if you are able to establish that our numbers are not accurate, then fine. However, we believe that they are accurate. We've had now three to four separate experts looking at these numbers.

President Trump: Certified accountants looked at them.

Kurt Hilbert: Correct. And this is just based on USPS data and your own secretary of state data. So that's what we would entreat and ask you to do. To sit down with us in a compromise and settlements proceeding and actually go through the registered voter IDs and the registrations. And if you can convince us that 24,149 is inaccurate, then fine. But we tend to believe that is, you know, obviously more than 11,779. That's sufficient to change the results entirely in and of itself. So what would you say to that, Mr. Germany?

Ryan Germany: I'm happy to get with our lawyers, and we'll set that up. That number is not accurate. And I think we can show you, for all the ones we've looked at, why it's not. And so if that would be helpful, I'm happy to get with our lawyers and set that up with you guys.

President Trump: Well, let me ask you, Kurt, you think that is an accurate number. That was based on the information given to you by the secretary of state's department, right?

Kurt Hilbert: That is correct. That information is the minimum, most conservative data based upon the USPS data and the secretary of state's office data that has been made publicly available. We do not have the internal numbers from the secretary of state. Yet we have asked for it six times. I sent a letter over to … several times requesting this information, and it's been rebuffed every single time. So it stands to reason that if the information is not forthcoming, there's something to hide. That's the problem that we have.

Ryan Germany: Well, that's not the case, sir. There are things that you guys are entitled to get. And there's things that under law, we are not allowed to give out.

President Trump: Well, you have to. Well, under law, you're not allowed to give faulty election results, okay? You're not allowed to do that. And that's what you done. This is a faulty election result. And honestly, this should go very fast. You should meet tomorrow because you have a big election coming up, and because of what you've done to the president— You know, the people of Georgia know that this was a scam— And because of what you've done to the president, a lot of people aren't going out to vote. And a lot of Republicans are going to vote negative because they hate what you did to the president. Okay? They hate it. And they're going to vote.

And you would be respected. Really respected, if this thing could be straightened out before the election. You have a big election coming up on Tuesday. And I think that it is really is important that you meet tomorrow and work out on these numbers. Because I know, Brad, that if you think we're right, I think you're going to say, and I'm not looking to blame anybody, I'm just saying, you know, and, you know, under new counts, and under new views, of the election results, we won the election. You know? It's very simple. We won the election. As the governors of major states and the surrounding states said, there is no way you lost Georgia. As the Georgia politicians say, there is no way you lost Georgia. Nobody. Everyone knows I won it by hundreds of thousands of votes. But I'll tell you it's going to have a big impact on Tuesday if you guys don't get this thing straightened out fast.

Mark Meadows: Mr. President, this is Mark. It sounds like we've got two different sides agreeing that we can look at those areas, and I assume that we can do that within the next twenty-four to forty-eight hours, to go ahead and get that reconciled so that we can look at the two claims and making sure that we get the access to the secretary of state's data to either validate or invalidate the claims that have been made. Is that correct?

Ryan Germany: No, that's not what I said. I'm happy to have our lawyers sit down with Kurt and the lawyers on that side and explain to him, hey, here's, based on what we've looked at so far, here's how we know. This is wrong. This is wrong. This is wrong. This is wrong. This is wrong.

Mark Meadows: So what you're saying, Ryan, let me let me make sure ... so what you're saying is you really don't want to give access to the data. You just want to make another case on why the lawsuit is wrong?

Ryan Germany: I don't think we can give access to data that's protected by law. But we can sit down with them and say—

President Trump: But you're allowed to have a phony election? You're allowed to have a phony election, right?

Ryan Germany: No, sir.

President Trump: When are you going to do signature counts, when are you going to do signature verification on Fulton County, which you said you were going to do. And now all of a sudden, you're not doing it. When are you doing that?

Ryan Germany: We are going to do that. We've announced—

Kurt Hilbert: To get to this issue of the personal information and privacy issue, is it possible that the secretary of state could deputize the lawyers for the president so that we could access that information and private information without you having any kind of violation?

President Trump: Well, I don't want to know who it is. You guys can do it very confidentially. You can sign a confidentiality agreement. That's okay. I don't need to know names. But on this stuff that we're talking about, we got all that information from the secretary of state.

Mark Meadows: Yeah. So let me let me recommend, Ryan, if you and Kurt will get together, you know, when we get off of this phone call, if you could get together and work out a plan to address some of what we've got with your attorneys where we can we can actually look at the data. For example, Mr. Secretary, I can you say there were only two dead people who would vote.

I can promise you there are more than that. And that may be what your investigation shows, but I can promise you there are more than that. But at the same time, I think it's important that we go ahead and move expeditiously to try to do this and resolve it as quickly as we possibly can. And if that's the good next step. Hopefully we can, we can finish this phone call and go ahead and agree that the two of you will get together immediately.

President Trump: Well, why don't my lawyers show you where you got the information. It will show the secretary of state, and you don't even have to look at any names. We don't want names. We don't care. But we got that information from you. And Stacey Abrams is laughing about you. She's going around saying these guys are dumber than a rock. What she's done to this party is unbelievable, I tell you. And I only ran against her once. And that was with a guy named Brian Kemp, and I beat her. And if I didn't run, Brian wouldn't have had even a shot, either in the general or in the primary. He was dead, dead as a doornail. He never thought he had a shot at either one of them. What a schmuck I was. But that's the way it is. That's the way it is.

I would like you … for the attorneys … I'd like you to perhaps meet with Ryan, ideally tomorrow, because I think we should come to a resolution of this before the election. Otherwise you're going to have people just not voting. They don't want to vote. They hate the state, they hate the governor, and they hate the secretary of state. I will tell you that right now. The only people that like you are people that will never vote for you. You know that, Brad, right? They like you, you know. They like you. They can't believe what they found. They want more people like you. So, look, can you get together tomorrow? And, Brad, we just want the truth. It's simple.

And everyone's going to look very good if the truth comes out. It's okay. It takes a little while, but let the truth come out. And the real truth is, I won by 400,000 votes. At least. That's the real truth. But we don't need 400,000 votes. We need less than 2,000 votes. And are you guys able to meet tomorrow, Ryan?

> *Observation: There were 5 million votes cast in Georgia. For President Trump to win by 400,000 as he stated, this would mean it was a 54 percent to 46 percent election. He's claiming he won Georgia in a landslide.*

Ryan Germany: I'll get with Chris, the lawyer who's representing us in the case, and see when he can get together with Kurt.

Brad Raffensperger: Ryan will be in touch with the other attorney on this call, Mr. Meadows. Thank you, President Trump, for your time.

President Trump: Okay, thank you, Brad. Thank you, Ryan. Thank you. Thank you, everybody. Thank you very much. Bye.

CHAPTER 10

THE AFTERMATH: OUR HOPE

I WAS DISAPPOINTED BUT NOT SURPRISED the following morning, January 3, when President Trump tweeted a misleading characterization of our phone call. I had not expected to mention the call publicly. I thought it was a private conversation. But he went public with it when he put out a tweet, and his tweet was false.

> I spoke to Secretary of State Brad Raffensperger yesterday about Fulton County and voter fraud in Georgia. He was unwilling, or unable, to answer questions such as the "ballots under table" scam, ballot destruction, out of state "voters", dead voters, and more. He has no clue![148]

I felt compelled to tweet a response.

Respectfully, President Trump: What you're saying is
not true. The truth will come out.[149]

I respect the positional authority of the president of the United
States, no matter who is sitting in the Oval Office, but my primary
responsibility as secretary of state is to oversee and protect Georgia's
elections.

President Trump was attempting to overturn the will of Georgia's
voters, and my duty was to prevent that from happening.

My instrument was truth.

Every day, I spoke the truth of Georgia's election results. My staff
and I had a tiny platform compared with President Trump's, and we
often felt swamped and discouraged when his disinformation was
magnified and retold.

The Washington Post placed a story about the call on their website
on Sunday night with a link to the recording.[150]

On Monday morning, a producer from *60 Minutes* called and
asked if I would be willing to be interviewed. They were putting
together a segment based on President Trump's call. When I was
growing up, our Sunday afternoon/evening ritual was to watch NFL
football and then *60 Minutes*. I guess nobody expects that call—least
of all me. We scheduled a time for the interview later in the week.

On Monday night, the last chance for Senators Perdue and
Loeffler to motivate their voters to vote on Tuesday, President Trump
headlined a rally for them in northwest Georgia. The president spoke
for more than an hour and mentioned "your secretary of state" more
often than he mentioned either candidate by name.

It was an incredible missed opportunity to promote Georgia's
two Republican U.S. senators.

Election Day turnout for the Senate runoff was 30 percent higher
than on November 3. With a total turnout of 4.4 million, more than
1.3 million voted at the polls. Voting progressed smoothly across

the state, and when the votes were tabulated, Georgia's Republican incumbents had both lost.

The new congress had been sworn in on January 3, ending Senator Perdue's term before the runoff. Senator Loeffler, however, had been appointed in 2019 to fill the seat of retired Senator Johnny Isakson, so she would serve until her successor was sworn in on January 20.

Then on Wednesday, January 6, recognizing that Congress was meeting in the afternoon to count and certify the electoral college votes, I drafted a letter to our Georgia Republican congressional delegation with a point-by-point rebuttal of the spurious allegations that the outcome of the Georgia vote was wrong. I signed the letter just after noon and transmitted it to our representatives.

I was hopeful to think a final presentation of the facts might change the minds of all, or even most, of them. They knew the truth. They knew that the election was not "stolen." They also believed their political futures depended on Donald Trump's continued support, and Trump's support mattered more to them than the truth.

A small "Stop the Steal" rally gathered outside the State Capitol, and some of the participants carried assault rifles. When one of the protesters, a former Ku Klux Klan leader who now leads American Patriots USA, entered the Capitol (unarmed) looking for me, the State Patrol decided it would be best if I left, and they escorted me out.

I did not know until I arrived home that the U.S. Capitol was under assault.

My letter to our Republican congressional delegation follows:

Office of the Secretary of State

Brad Raffensperger
SECRETARY OF STATE

January 6, 2021

VIA ELECTRONIC MAIL

The Honorable Jody Hice
404 Cannon House Office Building
Washington, D.C. 20515

The Honorable Barry Loudermilk
2133 Rayburn House Office Building
Washington, D.C. 20515

The Honorable Kelly Loeffler
131 Russell Senate Office Building
Washington, D.C. 20510

RE: Point by Point Refutation of False Claims about Georgia Elections

Dear Congressmen and Senator Loeffler:

Thank you to each of you for your service to our country. I am addressing this letter to you because each of you have publicly stated that you are going to object to Georgia's electors elected in the November 2020 election. You are certainly entitled to your opinions. However, I want to ensure that your colleagues in the House and Senate have accurate information on which to base their votes to your objection. I respectfully request that you enter this letter into the Congressional Record. Once these refutations are considered, I am confident that Georgia's validly elected electors will be accepted.

Like you, I am disappointed in the results of the 2020 Presidential Election. However, my office has taken multiple steps to confirm that the result is accurate, including conducting a hand audit that confirmed the results of the Presidential contest, a recount requested by President Trump that also confirmed the result, an audit of voting machines that confirmed the software on the machine was accurate and not tampered with, and an audit of absentee ballot signatures in Cobb County that confirmed that process was done correctly. Law enforcement officers with my office and the Georgia Bureau of Investigation have been diligently investigating all claims of fraud or irregularities and continue to investigate. Their work has shown me that there is nowhere close to sufficient

Letter to Congress
January 6, 2021
Page **2** of **10**

evidence to put in doubt the result of the presidential contest in Georgia. In Georgia, elections are run by county election officials in each of our 159 counties. While there is no such thing as a perfect election, our law enforcement officers are not seeing anything out of the ordinary scope of regular post-election issues that will be addressed by the State Election Board after the investigations are complete. There will end up being a small amount of illegal votes (there always is in any election because federal and state law err on the side of letting people vote and punishing them after the fact), but nowhere near the amount that would put the result of the presidential election in question.

The result of the presidential election is not what I preferred, but the result from Georgia is accurate. Indeed, this body, and both of you, have already voted to accept the results of Georgia's elections by voting to seat the elected Congressional representatives from Georgia. As your colleague Representative Chip Roy astutely pointed out, "[T]hose representatives were elected through the very same systems --- with the same ballot procedures, with the same signature validations, with the same broadly applied decisions of executive and judicial branch officials --- as were the electors chosen for the President of the United States under the laws of those states, which have become the subject of national controversy." Just as the result of your own election was valid and accurate, the certified result in the presidential contest is valid and accurate as well.

Losing candidates contesting election results and procedures is nothing new in Georgia. Former gubernatorial candidate Stacey Abrams and her allies made false claims about Georgia's election equipment and processes in the run up to and aftermath of her 2018 defeat. Many of those same claims are made now by the President and his allies. They were false then and are false now. Objecting to a state's presidential electors is nothing new in Congress either. Your colleagues on the other side of the aisle objected to accepting the votes of certain presidential electors after the 2000, 2004, and 2016 presidential elections. Those objections were not merited then, and, at least in the case of Georgia's electors, are not merited now. As Senator Tom Cotton recently pointed out, "If Congress purported to overturn the results of the Electoral College, it would not only exceed [it's] power, but also establish unwise precedents. ...Objecting to certified electoral votes won't give [President Trump] a second term—it will only embolden those Democrats who want to erode further our system of constitutional government."

POINT BY POINT REFUTATION OF FALSE CLAIMS

The claims raised by the President and his allies to dispute the result in Georgia fall into four broad categories: 1) allegations regarding Dominion voting machines, 2) allegations regarding absentee ballots, 3) allegations regarding poll watchers, and 4) allegations of votes cast by ineligible voters. I will go through each of the allegations in turn and explain how we know that none of these issues come even close to placing in doubt the result of the election.

214 State Capitol • Atlanta, Georgia • 30334 • Tel: (470) 312-2808

I.   ALLEGATIONS REGARDING DOMINION VOTING MACHINES

Many false allegations have been made about the Dominion voting machines. These claims were made by Democrat-allied groups prior to the election and are being made by people allied with the President now. These claims ranged from the perennial allegations from losing candidates that the machines were "flipping-votes" to the truly bizarre claims that Dominion was founded by foreign oligarchs and dictators for the purpose of keeping Hugo Chavez in power. The claims were false when Democrat-allied groups raised them prior to the election and are still false. These claims have been thoroughly debunked by election authorities, subject matter experts, and third party fact checkers.[1] There was even a social media rumor that a third-party had conducted an audit of voting machines in Ware County, Georgia and had found that the machines "flipped" votes from Trump to Biden at a rate of 28%. Not a single part of that rumor was true. It was quickly debunked by the Ware County Elections Director[2] and by fact checkers.[3] After Fox News and Newsmax were made aware that they had been reporting false claims about Dominion voting machines, both networks published retractions. Newsmax stated, "[n]o evidence has been offered that Dominion... used software of reprogrammed software that manipulated votes in the 2020 election."[4]

The allegations about Dominion most relevant to the election outcome in Georgia are that votes tallied on a Dominion vote tabulator were somehow manipulated on a statewide basis to elevate the count in favor of the Democratic presidential candidate. It is important to understand that this is not possible—not on a machine-by-machine basis, not by alleged hacking, not by manipulating software, and not by imagined ways of "sending" votes to overseas locations.[5] In Georgia, we were able to show that none of these allegations are true because we completed a 100% hand audit of all ballots cast in the presidential contest.[6] This hand audit, which relied exclusively on the printed text on

---

[1]Setting the Record Straight: Facts and Rumors. <https://www.dominionvoting.com/election2020-setting-the-record-straight/>. Accessed January 5, 2021.
[2] Ware County Election Supervisor Carlos Nelson said, "I can tell you this—I don't want to cuss—this is a darned lie. Our vote machines are secure. There's no vote flips."
https://sos.ga.gov/index.php/elections/secretary_of_states_office_debunks_ware_county_voting_machine_s tory. Accessed January 5, 2021.
[3] Dominion Machines Didn't Flip Votes in Ware County, Georgia. Associated Press. December 7, 2020.
https://apnews.com/article/fact-checking-9773239691. Accessed January 5, 2021.
[4]Fox News, Newsmax Shoot Down Their Own Aired Claims on Election After Threat of Legal Action.
USA Today. December 22, 2020. https://www.usatoday.com/story/entertainment/tv/2020/12/22/fox-newsmax-shoot-down-their-own-aired-claims-election/4004912001/. Accessed January 5, 2021.
[5] Dominion Statement on Sidney Powell Charges. <https://www.dominionvoting.com/dominion-statement-on-sidney-powell-charges/> . Accessed January 5, 2021.
[6]Georgia Secretary of State. Historic First Statewide Audit of Paper Ballots Upholds Results.
https://sos.ga.gov/index.php/elections/historic_first_statewide_audit_of_paper_ballots_upholds_result_of_p residential_race. Accessed January 5, 2021.

Letter to Congress
January 6, 2021
Page **4** of **10**

the ballot-marking device ballot or the bubbled in choice of the absentee ballot confirmed the result of the election with a 0% risk limit.[7]

We further know these allegations are false because our office engaged a federally-certified voting systems test lab to perform an audit of the voting machines following the November election.[8] Pro V&V, based in Huntsville, Alabama is a U.S. Election Assistance Commission-certified[9] Voting System Test Laboratory (VSTL), meaning the lab is "qualified to test voting systems to Federal standards."[10] Pro V&V's accreditation by the USEAC was also recommended by the National Institute of Standards and Technology (NIST), the U.S. government's physical science laboratory dedicated to creating standards and measures that would help America be the leading science innovator in the world.

Pro V&V conducted an audit of a random sample of Dominion Voting Systems voting machines throughout the state using forensic techniques, including equipment from Cobb, Douglas, Floyd, Morgan, Paulding, and Spalding Counties. ICP (precinct ballot scanners), ICX (ballot marking devices), and ICC (central absentee ballot scanners) components were all subject to the audit.[11] In conducting the audit, Pro V&V extracted the software or firmware from the components to check that the only software or firmware on the components was certified for use by the Secretary of State's office.[12] The testing was conducted on a Pro V&V laptop independent of the system.[13] According to the Pro V&V audit, all of the software and firmware on the sampled machines was verified to be the software and firmware certified for use by the Office of the Secretary of State.[14]

Through each of these actions, I can definitively say that the results reported by the Dominion Voting System used in Georgia were accurate.

II. ALLEGATIONS REGARDING ABSENTEE BALLOTS

Georgia has had no-excuse absentee voting since 2005, when it passed on a party-line vote by a Republican controlled legislature and was signed by a Republican governor. Traditionally, absentee by mail voting in Georgia only accounts for about 5% of the electorate, but due to the Coronavirus pandemic, it increased to approximately 25% of the electorate in November 2020. Absentee by mail ballots increased from around 222,000 in

---

[7] *Id.*

[8] Georgia Secretary of State. Secretary Raffensperger Accounces Completion of Voting Machine Audit. https://sos.ga.gov/index.php/elections/secretary_raffensperger_announces_completion_of_voting_machine _audit_using_forensic_techniques_no_sign_of_foul_play. Accessed January 5, 2021.

[9] https://www.eac.gov/voting-equipment/voting-system-test-laboratories-vstl/pro-vv

[10] *Id.*

[11] *See* Note 5, *supra.*

[12] *Id.*

[13] *Id.*

[14] *Id.*

Letter to Congress
January 6, 2021
Page **5** of **10**

the November 2018 General Election to over 1.3 million in the November 2020 Election. The President and his allies have alleged that Georgia did not adequately enforce its laws regarding verification of absentee ballots. This allegation is untrue. The truth is that my office protected and strengthened Georgia's signature verification system. My office provided GBI training to each county so that they could better conduct signature verification and also introduced a photo ID requirement into absentee ballot applications by creating an online request portal that requires the voter's name, date of birth, and Georgia driver's license number to match voter records in order to request an absentee ballot.

Much has been made of a Signature Match Settlement Agreement[15] entered into on the advice and recommendation of the Georgia Attorney General's office in order to protect Georgia's signature verification laws on both absentee ballots and absentee ballot applications. The President and his allies allege that the Settlement Agreement unconstitutionally changed Georgia law. That assertion has been rejected by courts and is not supported by the facts.

Multiple lawsuits have challenged the Settlement Agreement. All have rejected the claims that it weakened Georgia's signature match laws.[16] The Settlement Agreement came about because Democrat party groups filed a lawsuit challenging Georgia's signature verification process as unconstitutional. To get a full release of all claims and protect Georgia's signature verification laws, my office agreed to send out an Official Election Bulletin to counties from our Elections Director that offered best practices on how to conduct signature verification. The recommended practices were based off many counties' existing procedures.

As Judge Grimberg of the Northern District held in considering these claims, "[this] argument is belied by the record."[17] According to the latest data provided to our office from counties, Georgia counties rejected 2980 absentee ballots for missing or invalid signatures in the November election. This is in addition to the 2777 ballots that were initially identified as having a missing or invalid signature and were later cured by the voter pursuant to the process set forth by the Georgia General Assembly. Out of 1,322,529 absentee ballots cast in the November election, this means 0.43% of absentee ballots were initially identified as having a signature issue and that 0.22% of ballots were rejected due to missing or invalid signatures. These numbers are actually slightly higher than the number of rejected ballots for signature issues in the 2018 election, where

---

[15] The President and his allies generally refer to the Settlement Agreement as a Consent Order or Consent Decree. However, as the title of document clearly shows, it is a Compromise Settlement Agreement and Release.

[16] *See Wood v. Raffensperger et al.*, Order Denying TRO. NDGA. 1:20cv04651-SDG (stating that "Woods' argument is belied by the record.")

[17] *Id.*

Letter to Congress
January 6, 2021
Page **6** of **10**

222,193 absentee by mail ballots were cast and 454 were rejected for signature issues, a rejection rate of 0.2%.[18]

To further put any questions regarding Georgia county elections officials signature verification to bed, the law enforcement officers in my office, in conjunction with law enforcement officers with the Georgia Bureau of Investigation, conducted an audit of signatures on absentee ballots in Cobb County. We chose to start with Cobb County because it was the only county where the President and his allies had submitted any credible evidence that the signature verification process was not properly done. The audit found "no fraudulent absentee ballots" with a 99% confidence threshold (based on the sample size of reviewed signatures).[19] The audit found that only two ballots should have been identified by Cobb County Elections Officials for cure notification that weren't.[20] In one case, the ballot was "mistakenly signed by the elector's spouse," and in the other, the voter "reported signing the front of the envelope only."[21] In both cases, the identified voters filled out the ballots themselves.[22]

There have also been allegations of so-called "pristine ballots" in Fulton County. These are ballots that partisan poll watchers thought looked suspicious during the hand audit because they were not folded (as ballots that had been put in an envelope would be). First, there are numerous reasons why a hand-marked ballot may be not folded. Emergency ballots, which are ballots cast by eligible voters at polling places if there is an issue with a ballot marking device, are scanned straight into the scanner. Certain military/overseas ballots or ballots that are damaged and cannot be scanned are duplicated and would also not be folded prior to scanning. The unstated implication of this allegation is that county elections officials are creating fake or invalid ballots and running them through scanners. There is absolutely no evidence that this happened a single time in Georgia.

Finally, there have been allegations of illegal ballot harvesting. One of the first things I did as Secretary of State was to ensure that ballot harvesting was illegal in Georgia. The law outlawing ballot harvesting in Georgia was challenged in court, but we successfully defended it. No specific allegations of ballot harvesting have been brought forward. Nevertheless, the MITRE Corporation's National Election Security Lab conducted a statewide Ballot Harvesting Analysis of the November elections across Georgia's 159 counties. MITRE collected data on the absentee by mail ballots requested and returned to check for unusually high or unusually low return rates. According to the report, a

---

[18] *Id.*
[19] Georgia Secretary of State/Georgia Bureau of Investigation Absentee by Mail Signature Audit Report. December 29, 2020.
https://sos.ga.gov/admin/uploads/Cobb%20County%20ABM%20Audit%20Report%2020201229.pdf.
Accessed January 5, 2021.
[20] *Id.*
[21] *Id.*
[22] *Id.*

"statistical analysis of ballot return rates shows no anomalous points; no suspicious indicators of ballot harvesting."[23]

III. ALLEGATIONS REGARDING POLL WATCHERS

There have been numerous reports of insufficient access for poll watchers or public monitors. Ironically, those reports are all made by poll watchers or other public monitors, showing that they were in fact highly involved in the process and monitoring each step of the way. Georgia law balances access for partisan poll watchers and public observers with the necessity of allowing county election officials to complete their work in a timely fashion without interference. It is not unusual in any election for partisan poll watchers and election officials to disagree on the exact level of access that they should receive. Throughout this election cycle, my office has told Georgia counties to ensure transparency and openness and, when any questions arise, to err on the side of transparency. We ensured monitors had access and that the public could observe the hand audit and recount, in addition to the regular laws that govern partisan poll watchers on Election Day and early voting.[24]

The most prominent allegation of issues with monitors took place in State Farm Arena, where Fulton County conducted its absentee ballot processing. Unfortunately, due to what appears to be a miscommunication between county staff and poll watchers, the poll watchers left at 10:30 p.m. on election night when they thought Fulton was done scanning for the night. Fulton denies ever telling monitors that they had to leave. Fortunately, a monitor designated by the State Election Board arrived shortly after the other poll watchers left. Partisan poll watchers and other monitors remained at Fulton County's election warehouse where results were being tabulated the entire time and were aware that absentee ballot scanning was continuing at State Farm Arena. Fortunately, surveillance video of the entire time scanning was taking place exists and is publicly available. While the President and his allies have used snippets of that video to imply untoward activity, review of the entire surveillance tape by both law enforcement officers with my office and fact checkers has shown that no untoward activity took place— election officials simply scanned valid ballots as they had been doing all night. The entire video has been made available by my office so that people can confirm this fact for themselves.[25]

IV. ALLEGATIONS REGARDING INELIGBLE VOTERS VOTING

---

[23] Georgia Secretary of State. National Election Security Lab Report on November Election. https://sos.ga.gov/index.php/elections/national_election_security_lab_report_on_november_election_shows _sec_raffenspergers_ballot_harvesting_ban_holds_strong. Accessed January 5, 2021.
[24] Georgia Secretary of State. Monitors Closely Observing Audit Triggered Full Hand Recount. https://sos.ga.gov/index.php/elections/monitors_closely_observing_audit-triggered_full_hand_recount_transparency_is_built_into_process. Accessed January 5, 2021.
[25] SecureVote GA Fact Check. https://securevotega.com/factcheck/. Accessed January 5, 2021.

Letter to Congress
January 6, 2021
Page **8** of **10**

The President and his allies have also made allegations regarding ineligible voters voting. My office has investigated each of these allegations and will continue to investigate them, but our initial investigations show two things: 1) the data used by the President's allies is not correct and 2) the actual number of potentially ineligible voters who voted in Georgia does not put the result of the election in question.

There are ineligible voters who vote in every election because both federal and state law err on the side of letting a potentially eligible voter vote and then punish any illegal voting after the fact. If the number of illegal voters is sufficient to place the result in question, the remedy is an election contest filed in state court. The President and his allies have filed multiple election contests in Georgia. Three have already been dismissed, and one remains ongoing. In Georgia, we have strong laws to deter illegal voting, and we conduct as much list maintenance on our voter rolls as allowed by federal law.

The data that the President's allies used to determine their alleged number of illegal voters is wrong. Matt Braynard, the President's purported expert witness in his election contest, has already admitted in testimony to the Georgia House of Representatives Government Affairs Committee that he is not accusing the people he has identified of actually voting illegally.[26] Although he states in his affidavit filed in Court that there were 20,312 individuals who cast ballots illegally in the November 3, 2020 election..., he clarified to the Georgia House of Representatives Government Affairs Committee that he was not actually accusing anyone of voting illegally.[27] Actual experts in political science, data analysis, and election data have pointed out the data used by Mr. Braynard is not reliable. Dr. Charles Stewart III, the Kenan Sahin Distinguished Professor at the Massachusetts Institute of Technology and the founding director of the MIT Election Data and Science Lab, reviewed Mr. Braynard's declaration and data and concluded that he uses data matching techniques that are "[k]nown to be unreliable and produce a preponderance of 'false positives' and that the methodology used by Mr. Braynard and the President's other purported experts is "highly inaccurate."[28]

Despite the inaccuracy of the numbers alleged by the President's allies, my office is committed to fully investigating all claims of illegal voting, and that is exactly what we have been doing. Those investigations are tedious and time consuming because whether or not a person actually illegally voted can depend on the specific factual circumstances, but those investigations have allowed me to get a good sense of the potential universe of illegal voters in the November election in Georgia. The factual investigations confirm the

---

[26] *Trump v. Raffensperger*. Fulton County Superior Court. Civil Action No. 2020-CV343255. Respondent's Motion to Exclude Affidavits and Testimony of Experts. December 15, 2020.

[27] *Id.* Braynard Testimony to Georgia House of Representatives Government Affairs Committee. December 10, 2020. ("In my affidavit I don't believe I specifically accuse anybody of committing any crime. I said there were indications—over and over again potentially illegal ballots has been my language. Uh indications of illegally cast ballots. I have not accused anybody of committing a felony in any of my declarations.").

[28] *See* Note 25, *supra*. Declaration of Dr. Charles Stewart III.

214 State Capitol ● Atlanta, Georgia ● 30334 ● Tel: (470) 312-2808

opinions of experts like Dr. Stewart who have accurately concluded that the numbers of illegal voters in Georgia alleged by the President's allies are not accurate or reliable.

The President's allies have alleged that 2,056 felons voted illegally in Georgia. By comparing information from the Department of Corrections and Department of Community Supervision to the list of people who voted in November, the actual universe of potential felon voters is 74. Each of those voters are under investigation to determine if they are the same person indicated and that they are still under felony sentence.

The President's allies have alleged that 66,241 underage teenagers voted in Georgia in November. The actual number is 0. Our office compared the list of people who voted in Georgia to their full birthdays to determine this. 4 voters requested a ballot prior to turning 18, and all 4 turned 18 prior to the November 3 election.

The President's allies allege that 2,423 people voted who were not registered to vote. The actual number is 0. Voters cannot be given credit for voting in Georgia unless they are registered to vote.

The President's allies allege that 10,315 dead people voted. Our office has discovered 2 potential dead voters and both instances are under investigation. We will fully investigate all credible allegations of potential dead voters, but the allegation that a large number of dead people voted in Georgia is not supported by any evidence.

The President's allies allege that 395 people cast ballots in both Georgia and another state in November. That list is under investigation and in working with election officials from other states, we have already determined that many of the alleged "double voters" are not the same people.

The President's allies allege that 1,043 people voted who were registered at addresses that are actually post office boxes. A simple google search of this list revealed that many of the addresses that are alleged to be post office boxes are actually apartments. The President's allies allege that approximately 4000 people voted in Georgia who had subsequent voter registrations in other states. Our research into these people shows that these allegations rely on inaccurate and incomplete data. The detailed voter registration records on those voters reviewed so far show that they are legitimate Georgia voters. The President's allies also allege that there are approximately 15,000 people who voted in Georgia after having filed a National Change of Address with the U.S. Post Office indicating they had a new out of state address. Mr. Braynard himself admits this fact does not establish that a person voted illegally. There are many people who live out of state who are still completely legitimate Georgia residents, including military and overseas citizens, people in government service, college students, temporary workers on assignment somewhere else, and voters temporarily caring for family others, etc. There will end up being a small amount of illegal out-of-state voters, and my office will seek punishment for those voters to the full extent of the law. But our initial investigation

Letter to Congress
January 6, 2021
Page **10** of **10**

indicates that the total number of illegal voters for any reason (no longer a Georgia resident, felon, double voter, etc.) will not be close to sufficient to place the result of the presidential election in Georgia in question.

CONCLUSION

As Secretary of State of Georgia, I know that half the people are going to be happy after an election and the other half are going to be upset. My job is to make sure that both sides know that the results are accurate. That is why I ordered a hand audit, a recount, a signature audit in Cobb County, and a statewide signature study in conjunction with the University of Georgia. The facts show that the claims asserted by the President and his allies about the voting machines used in Georgia are false. The facts show that the claims that the 2020 election did not follow Georgia law on absentee ballots are false. The claims that the election was not transparent or that monitors did not have the access to which they were entitled are false. The claims that there are a sufficient number of illegal voters to put the result of the Presidential contest in question are false. You have already accepted the results of the November 3, 2020 election in Georgia for your own seats and those of your colleagues. I respectfully request that, after you review this evidence, you do the same for the presidential electors who were validly elected by the people of Georgia. We do not have to like the results of an election to accept them. Thank you for your consideration and your continued service to our country.

Sincerely,

Brad Raffensperger

cc: Georgia Congressional Delegation
        Office of the Vice President of the United States
        Office of the Speaker of the United States House of Representatives
        Office of the Minority Leader of the United States House of Representatives
        Office of the Majority Leader of the United States Senate
        Office of the Minority Leader of the United States Senate

Congress returned to a very different Capitol on Wednesday night. Despite the destruction and desecration, Rep. Jody Hice and five other Georgia Republican representatives continued to foment disinformation.[151] Hice stood before Congress and presented his objection to Georgia's electoral votes for President-elect Biden.

Ironically, Hice accepted the results of his own race, which he won, but objected to the results of the presidential race. Same voters. Same ballots. One, presumably, was honest. The other was "faulty and fraudulent." He's a double-minded person. How can you hold two opposing views at one time?

"Mr. President," Hice said, "myself, members of the Georgia delegation and some seventy-four of my Republican colleagues and I object to the electoral votes from the state of Georgia on the grounds the election conducted on November 3 was faulty and fraudulent due to unilateral actions by the secretary of state to unlawfully change the state's election process without approval from the General Assembly, thereby setting the stage for an unprecedented amount of fraud and irregularities, and I have signed the objection myself."

Vice President Mike Pence, chairing the session, told Hice, "Sections 15 and 17 of Title 3 of the United States Code require that any objection be presented in writing and signed by a member of the House of Representatives and a senator. Is the objection in writing and signed by a member and a senator?"

"Mr. President, prior to the actions and events of today we did," Hice said. "But following the events of today, it appears that some senators have withdrawn their objection."

"In that case," Pence said, "the objection cannot be entertained."

Senator Kelly Loeffler offered an explanation for her decision not to support Hice's objection:

Mr. President, when I arrived in Washington this morning, I fully intended to object to the certification of the electoral votes. However, the events that have transpired today have forced me to reconsider and I cannot now in good conscience object to the certifi-cation of these electors. The violence, the lawlessness and siege of the halls of Congress are abhorrent and stand as a direct attack on the very institution my objection was intended to protect, the sanctity of the American democratic process. And I thank law enforcement for keeping us safe. I believe that there were last minute changes to the November 2020 election process and serious irregularities that resulted in too many Americans losing confidence, not only in the integrity of our elections, but in the power of the ballot as a tool of democracy. Too many Americans are frustrated at what they see as an unfair system.

Nevertheless, there is no excuse for the events that took place in these chambers today. And I pray that America never suffers such a dark day again. Though the fate of this vote is clear, the future of the American people's faith in the core institution of this democracy remains uncertain.

We, as a body, must turn our focus to protecting the integrity of our elections and restoring every American's faith that their voice and their vote matters. America is a divided country with serious differences, but it is still the greatest country on earth. There can be no disagreement that upholding democracy is the only path to preserving our republic.

TRUMP AND SHAFER GIVE UP WITHOUT A FIGHT IN COURT

After weeks of rumors, it was time for the president's lawyers to go to court—put their witnesses under oath and swear that everything they had said was true. Their day in court was scheduled for Friday, January 8, before Cobb County Superior Court Judge Adele Grubbs.

Then on the eve of the opportunity they had been begging for, President Trump and Georgia Republican Party chairman David Shafer's legal team withdrew without a fight. They folded and volun-tarily dropped their remaining four lawsuits in Georgia rather than submit their evidence to a court and open themselves to cross-examination under oath. No judge. No jury.

I wrote on December 4, "If you want to know the truth, watch what happens in court." Because in court, witnesses who lie risk prison time, and lawyers who lie risk losing their license to practice.

We looked forward to meeting the president's lawyers in that forum. We knew we had the truth on our side.

The president's lawyers withdrew four cases on Thursday before their court date the following day:

- Trump v. Kemp (U.S. District Court for the Northern District of Georgia)
- Trump et al. v. Raffensperger et al. (Superior Court of Fulton County)
- Still v. Raffensperger et al. (Superior Court of Cobb County)
- Boland v. Raffensperger et al. (Supreme Court of Georgia)

All the president's tweets and all of his lawyers' press conferences and sliced-up videos had amounted to nothing, because they were unwilling to make those same claims to a judge or a jury. They walked away.

But even in capitulation, they continued to spread disinformation. The president's legal team falsely characterized the dismissal of their lawsuits as "due to an out-of-court settlement agreement." There was no settlement agreement. Correspondence sent to Trump's legal team prior to the dismissals, however, made clear that they quit. Gave up.

60 MINUTES TELLS THE STORY

On Sunday evening, Tricia and I sat down to watch 60 Minutes, with the second hand ticking and my face on the screen.[152]

"Raffensperger is a lifelong Republican," Scott Pelley said, introducing the segment, "voted for Mr. Trump and contributed to his campaign. But facing the president's wrath, he would not choose loyalty over duty."

Pelley and I discussed President Trump's phone call. I repeated what I had said to the president: "Well, Mr. President, the challenge that you have is that you have bad data. Our data shows that you did not win the race."

They played several clips from the call where the president claimed he won in Georgia and then said to me, "So, look. All I want to do is this. I just want to find 11,780 votes."

Pelley asked, "What was the president asking you to do?"

"He was asking us to recalibrate or recalculate, I believe it was, recalculate—somehow get a different answer. But I'm an engineer. And anyone that's good with numbers knows you can calculate all you want, but the numbers are the numbers."

Pelley also interviewed Gabe Sterling, who was much more direct in his language than I had been.[153] When Pelley asked Gabe about Rudy Giuliani's December 3 testimony to the Georgia state senate committee, Gabe said, "From my point of view, they intentionally misled the state senators, the people of Georgia, and the people of the United States about this to cause this conspiracy theory to keep going and keep the disinformation going, which has caused this environment that we're seeing today."

Pelley asked, "Are you saying they lied to the Georgia State Senate?"

"I'm saying that Rudy Giuliani looked them in the eye and lied."

"And Rudy Giuliani knows that," I said when Pelley asked me about Gabe's statement. "He also, I believe, you know, he has some ethical standards as a member of the bar. He knows that what he said was not true. But our State Senate did not ask us to come in there so that we could rebut what they said. And it was actually left as the gospel truth, and it wasn't. It was fabricated."

They also played a clip of President Trump at the January 6 rally before the Capitol was stormed: "No, it's amazing. The weak Republicans, they're pathetic Republicans . . ."

Then Pelley said, "When the president was making his speech on Wednesday, inciting that mob in Washington, he complained about weak and pathetic Republicans. He was talking about you."

"Well, I think he was talking about others," I responded. "I think actually I showed that I had some courage. I had some gumption. I actually would do my job. The ones that kowtow to him, that just bent over and did his bidding, and not looking into the facts, I think that's weakness."

They wrapped up the segment by asking me about the attack on the Capitol, and I reflected on the importance of knowing our nation's history. I was glad the *60 Minutes* producer included my comment in the final cut: "It was surreal. We've never seen anything like that in 150 years, maybe even longer, probably 200 years. It was really an affront to the people that founded this nation. People need to go back and read their history books. You know we had some great founders. I know they weren't perfect men, but they were great people. They were some of the most learned people we had in our society. And that's the high ideal that we all should elevate ourselves to be, noble people of high character, and patriotic, and love our country."[154]

REBUILDING TRUST

Our nation has spent more than two centuries building the safest, most secure election system in history. That system isn't static. To maintain security and to build voter trust, we continue to make changes. In Georgia, that meant in 2019 we bought new voting machines that created a paper ballot for voters to confirm their selections with a paper-based audit trail. At the same time, Georgia eliminated ballot harvesting, which had led to fraud in at least one other state and allowed legal voters with proper identification to "cure" a problem with a signature on an absentee ballot.

I also secured authority from the General Assembly for the state of Georgia to join the Electronic Registration Information Center ("ERIC"), a voluntary state-led and operated multistate voter information sharing service. Today, more than thirty states have joined, red and blue ones, and all are welcome, because the goal is for every state to have up-to-date, clean voter registration lists. All of our Southeastern states except Tennessee have joined. ERIC has tremendous data tracking of death records and provides updates to every state when citizens move from one ERIC member state to another, so we can update our voters rolls objectively more consistently, accurately, and often.

And in 2021, we added an identification requirement for absentee voters that matches what federal law requires for people who register to vote by mail. We also added a requirement that counties utilize early processing of absentee ballots to ensure that results can be posted quicker and made other improvements to ensure smoother administration of elections.

Each of these updates was an improvement to the system and an attempt to build trust that we have honest, fair elections with the appropriate balance of accessibility and security.

Yet we stand at this moment when millions of Americans say they do not trust the outcome of our recent elections. What they are literally saying, both Democrats and Republicans, is that they don't trust the outcome of elections *when they lose.*

Repairing that problem goes deeper than voting machines.

CHARACTER COUNTS

The real issue is not complex; it's very straightforward. We are wasting our time talking about vision, goals, and policies if we don't address the key issue: character. If we don't have people of the highest character run for elected office, we will continue to fight disinformation, misinformation, and outright deception, and the end result will be an erosion of public trust. We need the people who hold public office to continually strive for the noble causes in life with noble behavior. Let's move upward so we can move forward.

When you eat your young and you go after people in your own party who are loyal, traditional Republicans, you are destroying our future as a party. It was Reagan himself who said, "The person who agrees with you 80 percent of the time is a friend and an ally—not a 20 percent traitor." Politics is all about addition, and on a great day, multiplication. It's about staying true to your principles and welcoming others to join our grand march for our common vision.

In my lifetime, two presidents have been revered above others: Ronald Reagan and John F. Kennedy. Reagan and Kennedy were not universally loved, of course, nor even universally liked. Even in his overwhelming defeat of Walter Mondale in 1984, more than 37 million Americans voted against Reagan, but Reagan's forty-nine-state Electoral College victory is one for the history books. Mondale only carried his home state of Minnesota. Now that's a mandate.

Both men had charisma, a good sense of humor, and very good communication skills, but their ability to connect was more complex than that.

Reagan summed up his approach to life in the statement, "Live simply, love generously, care deeply, speak kindly, leave the rest to God."

He was called "The Great Communicator" in large part because his communication style reflected his optimistic outlook about America and Americans. He wrapped his message in charm and grace that endeared him to millions.

He believed much of what gets accomplished is due to great teamwork, whether in business, politics, religion, or just daily living. "There is no limit to the amount of good you can do if you don't care who gets the credit," he said.

Reagan was confident in two things: himself and the American people. He could liberally share the limelight with anyone because he was comfortable in himself. That gave him the confidence to negotiate with the Russians, other foreign powers, and very importantly, the key leaders on the other side of the aisle. Stories of Reagan's weekly lunches with Democratic Speaker of the House Tip O'Neill have been told so many times that mentioning them here risks coming across as trite. But we cannot forget these two men loved America and Americans and were willing to set aside their egos for the sake of the entire country to get something done. And they did!

Today, Republicans and Democrats are afraid to sit down with the other side because their colleagues will think they're selling out to the other side. Even trying to hear what someone in the other party has to say is viewed as a sign of weakness.

In the construction business, when we have a dispute but can see no way to resolve it, we opt for mediation and arbitration. We sit down to discuss our differences. It's cheaper, more effective, and a better use of our most precious resource—time—to negotiate.

Before we get into strategies and tactics, the issue of character goes to the core of the problem. When we have people of good character in elected office, a lot of issues will begin to work themselves out.

Character consists of several intertwined elements: integrity, values, truthfulness, moral courage, and all those other positive attributes that we innately respect in a person.

Integrity counts. It always will. Like you, I'm a regular American who had to make a choice. I chose integrity and the truth. We all have decision points in our life. If you haven't already, you will come to that proverbial fork in the road someday and have to make the same decision—do what is right, or choose what is expedient. Recently, a pastor, who happens to be a Republican, told me that "moral cowardice has injected embalming fluid into our future." It was a strong, graphic statement.

The truth I have shared in this book is supported by the facts. I stated early in this book that it would be difficult for people on both sides of the political spectrum to hear. I have written this book for people for who want to know and understand how we got to this point in America where a sizeable segment of Americans from both sides of the aisle don't trust the election process and the results. It didn't start in 2020, and Georgia, interestingly enough, plays a key role in this national drama.

During the post-election chaos, my son Kyle quietly shared a great piece of wisdom with me: "No one can beat the river back, but we can control its direction." The power in that statement is the "we." We is you and me. We the people. Our Founders would expect no less from us, and our children are watching to see if our actions match our words.

ACKNOWLEDGMENTS

I am grateful for everyone who has positively touched my life over the years. First and foremost is Tricia, my high school sweetheart and wife of forty-five years. I love her and cherish our life together, and I am very thankful that over the years our hearts have melded into one. She is incredibly kind, joyful, and filled with energy. Her laugh is engaging, and her smile has warmed my heart since day one. She is my biggest supporter, and I am hers.

I love my boys, who are now grown men. Each of my sons has his unique gifts—courage, steadfastness, humor, kindness, and loyalty. I am grateful that they each taught me lessons for life. I am thankful for the women my sons have married. They are loving and kind and have expanded our family with joy.

I am very grateful I have the blessing of grandchildren. I love their sense of wonder, adventure, and joy of living. Grandchildren are our hope for a better future, and they reinforce for me my desire to finish well and strong.

And all of what I have become was the foundation and values that my parents spoke into my life growing up. Traditional values like honesty, character, and respect.

My friends have been a blessing, and I am grateful for the small men's groups from church and the business world who spoke encouragement, truth, and accountability into my life.

I am also grateful that on my journey of faith I had the blessing of pastors in Manassas, Lilburn, Johns Creek, and Alpharetta.

As a business owner, I am grateful for our team of dedicated and loyal professionals. A company is only as great as the people who are members of the team, and we have superb talent in our organization.

In the Office of Secretary of State, I am blessed beyond measure with our entire team. My Deputy Secretary of State Jordan Fuchs, Chief Operating Officer Gabriel Sterling, and General Counsel Ryan Germany have been in the crosshairs with me and took on more attacks than anyone should have had to withstand. Through it all, they did not flinch and stood with me and for the truth. I greatly appreciate your courage and loyalty.

Our front office staff and election team and investigators also took more than their share of incoming flak and I am grateful you did not wilt.

To the good people of Georgia and indeed all corners of America who wrote to me and my staff words of encouragement, emailed me, shared your favorite Bible verses, sent us flowers and other uplifting gestures, I want to let you know how much that meant to me, our team, and Tricia. Thank you!

To the good people of Georgia who placed your trust in me in 2018 to be your Georgia secretary of state, I am grateful for your kindness and support.

Above all, I want to acknowledge Christ, my savior. My faith defines who I am and who I have become. It is what beckons me to strive upward in my speech and my actions.

With deep gratitude,

Brad Raffensperger
June 2021

NOTES

1   The Save America March, Washington, D.C., January 6, 2021.

2   Lauren Groh-Wargo (@gwlauren), "It is not the time for false equivalencies," Twitter, December 6, 2020, https://twitter.com/gwlauren/status/1335618120006955015.

3   "First Inaugural Address of Ronald Reagan," January 20, 1981, https://www.reaganfoundation.org/ronald-reagan/reagan-quotes-speeches/inaugural-address-1/.

4   GA Secretary of State Raffensperger ®: Focused on having safe voting process," *Cavuto Live*, Fox News, January 2, 2021.

5   Ibid.

6   Ibid.

7   Inaugural Address of Governor Nathan Deal, January 10, 2011, https://nathandeal.georgia.gov/press-releases/2011-01-10/inaugural-address-governor-nathan-deal/.

8   Ronald Sullivan, "Ben Fortson Jr. Is Dead at 74; Ex-Secretary of State in Georgia," *The New York Times*, May 21, 1979, https://www.nytimes.com/1979/05/21/archives/ben-fortson-jr-is-dead-at-74-exsecretary-of-state-in-georgia.html.

9   Richard Fausset, "Lasting Rancor Over Voting Issues Puts a Spotlight on a Georgia Runoff," *The New York Times*, November 30, 2018, https://www.nytimes.com/2018/11/30/us/voting-rights-georgia-runoff.html.

10   Brad Raffensperger, "Ga. Needs Fair, Open, Accurate, Secure Elections," The Atlanta Journal-Constitution, November 19, 2018, https://www.ajc.com/news/opinion/opinion-needs-fair-open-accurate-secure-elections/xCMoIw0E1XgS9N-2RQ6ri4J/.

11   "Secure, Accessible & Fair Elections (SAFE) Commission Report Submitted to the General Assembly," January 10, 2019, https://sos.ga.gov/admin/uploads/SAFE_Commission_Report_FINAL_(1-10-18).pdf.

12   Claudia Wallis, "Trump's Victory and the Politics of Resentment," *Scientific American*, November 12, 2016, https://www.scientificamerican.com/article/trump-s-victory-and-the-politics-of-resentment/.

13   Brad Raffensperger, "The Assault on Trust in Our Elections," National Affairs, Spring 2021, https://nationalaffairs.com/publications/detail/the-assault-on-trust-in-our-elections.

14   Common Cause v. Kemp, 1:18-CV-5102-AT, Transcript of Hearing on Motion for Temporary Restraining Order, November 8, 2018.

15   Donald J. Trump (@realDonaldTrump), Twitter, November 6, 2012, See archive at: https://www.thetrumparchive.com/?results=1&searchbox=%22total+sham+and+a+travesty%22.

16   Gregory Krieg, "Sound Familiar Trump Called 2012 Vote a 'Total Sham,'" CNN Politics, October 20, 2016, https://www.cnn.com/2016/10/18/politics/donald-trump-rigged-vote-twitter-2012/index.html.

17   Donald J. Trump (@realDonaldTrump), Twitter, November 6, 2012, See archive at: https://www.thetrumparchive.com/?results=1&searchbox=%22we+should+march+on+washington%22.

18   Donald J. Trump (@realDonaldTrump), Twitter, November 6, 2012, See archive at: https://www.thetrumparchive.com/?results=1&searchbox=%22lets+fight+like+hell%22.

19   Rosie Gray, "Paul Ryan 'Fully Confident' Election Will Be Carried Out Fairly, Spokesperson Says," BuzzFeed.News, October 15, 2016, https://www.buzzfeednews.com/article/rosiegray/paul-ryan-fully-confident-election-will-be-carried-out-fairl.

20   Aaron Blake, "Democrats Are Now Going There on 'Stolen' Elections," *The Washington Post*, November 15, 2018, https://www.washingtonpost.com/politics/2018/11/15/democrats-are-now-going-there-stolen-elections/.

21   Hunter Walker, "Cory Booker says the Georgia election is being 'stolen' from Stacey Abrams," *Yahoo!news*, November 13, 2018, https://www.yahoo.com/news/cory-booker-says-georgia-election-stolen-stacey-abrams-012932105.html.

22   Jonathan Tilove, "In Austin, Hillary Clinton honored for public service," *Statesman*, November 13, 2018, https://www.statesman.com/news/20181113/in-austin-hillary-clinton-honored-for-public-service.

23   Ibid.

24   Jon Ward, "How Stacey Abrams became the 'architect' of Biden's Georgia surge," *Yahoo!news*, November 6, 2020, https://www.yahoo.com/now/georgia-election-results-trump-biden-140754054.html.

25   Khushbu Shah, "'Textbook voter suppression': Georgia's bitter election a battle years in the making," *The Guardian*, November 10, 2018, https://www.theguardian.com/us-news/2018/nov/10/georgia-election-recount-stacey-abrams-brian-kemp.

26   Ryan Bort, "Judges Are Doing All They Can to Keep Brian Kemp from Stealing the Georgia Election," *Rolling Stone*, November 13, 2018, https://www.rollingstone.com/politics/politics-news/brian-kemp-georgia-votes-755280/.

27   Vann R. Newkirk II, "The Georgia Governor's Race Has Brought Voter Suppres-

sion Into Full View," *The Atlantic*, November 6, 2018, https://www.theatlantic.com/politics/archive/2018/11/how-voter-suppression-actually-works/575035/.

28   Nick Corasaniti and Reid J. Epstein, "What Georgia's Voting Law Really Does, *The New York Times*, April 2, 2021, https://www.nytimes.com/2021/04/02/us/politics/georgia-voting-law-annotated.html.

29   "The Mythology of Voter Suppression," *The Wall Street Journal*, November 22, 2019, https://www.wsj.com/articles/the-mythology-of-voter-suppression-11574467350.

30   Greg Bluestein and Maya T. Prabhu, "LIVE UPDATES: Biden, Buttigieg say voter suppression cost Abrams 2018 election," *The Atlanta Journal-Constitution*, June 10, 2019, https://www.ajc.com/blog/politics/live-updates-biden-beto-buttigieg-and-booker-campaign-atlanta/Pilo4U0aRgUGDLPA3BhIhK/.

31   Jay Caruso, "If you called out Donald Trump for dismissing democracy in 2016, you should call out Stacey Abrams and Mayor Pete today," *Independent*, June 7, 2019, https://www.independent.co.uk/voices/pete-buttigieg-stacey-abrams-georgia-election-trump-2016-joe-biden-elizabeth-warren-a8949541.html.

32   Reid Wilson, "Stacey Abrams PAC Tops $100 Million Raised," The Hill, July 9, 2021, https://thehill.com/homenews/campaign/562298-stacey-abrams-pac-tops-100-million-raised.

33   "Fair Fight Action and Care in Action v. Robyn A. Crittenden, et al.," Courthousenews.com, https://www.courthousenews.com/wp-content/uploads/2018/11/GEORGIA-Fair-Fight-Complaint.pdf.

34   Charles Bethea, "Stacey Abrams Ends Her Race for Governor of Georgia, but Doesn't Quote Concede," *The New Yorker*, November 16, 2018, https://www.newyorker.com/news/current/stacey-abrams-ends-her-race-for-governor-of-georgia-but-doesnt-quite-concede.

35   Case 1:20-cv-01986-ELR, Democracydocket.com: https://www.democracydocket.com/wp-content/uploads/sites/45/2020/07/PI-Order-GA-4-Pillars.pdf.

36   "Presidential Preference Primary Delayed; Will Be Held with General Primary in May," The News-Reporter," March 18, 2020, https://www.news-reporter.com/articles/presidential-preference-primary-delayed-will-be-held-with-general-primary-in-may/.

37   Stephanie Saul, "Georgia Postpones Its Primary as Virus Upends Voting," *The New York Times*, March 14, 2020, https://www.nytimes.com/2020/03/14/us/politics/georgia-primary-virus-2020.html.

38   Amanda Terkel, "Georgia GOP Leader: More Absentee Voting Will Help Turnout, Be 'Devastating to Republicans,'" *Huffpost*, April 2, 2020, https://www.huffpost.com/entry/georgia-absentee-voting-republicans-david-ralston_n_5e85f-736c5b692780508d69f.

39   Jonathan Easley, "Georgia Makes It Easier to Get Mail-in Ballots after Delaying Primary," *The Hill*, March 24, 2020, https://thehill.com/homenews/campaign/489245-georgia-expanding-access-to-mail-in-ballots-after-delaying-primary.

40   Mark Niesse, "Georgia Primary Delayed Again to June 9 During Coronavirus Emergency," *The Atlanta Journal-Constitution*, April 9, 2020, https://

www.ajc.com/news/state--regional-govt--politics/georgia-primary-de-layed-again-june-during-coronavirus-emergency/W5ElsYWTsP5clpNAVTYX-nO/.

41   Ibid.

42   Donald J. Trump (@realDonaldTrump), Twitter, May 26, 2020, See archive at: https://www.thetrumparchive.com/?results=1&searchbox-=%22NO+WAY+%28ZERO%21%29+that+Mail-in%22.

43   Mark Niesse, "Voting Machines and Coronavirus Force Long Lines on Georgia Voters," *The Atlanta Journal-Constitution*, June 9, 2020, https://www.ajc.com/news/state--regional-govt--politics/voting-machines-and-coronavirus-force-long-lines-georgia-voters/VajM2D3aSHALhCz7KwDrpJ/.

44   "State Election Board Refers Fulton Absentee Mishandling Case to Georgia Attorney General," https://sos.ga.gov/index.php/elections/state_election_board_refers_fulton_absentee_mishandling__case_to_georgia_attorney_general.

45   Kate Brumback, "Judge: Postage requirement for mail ballot isn't a poll tax," *The Associated Press*, August 11, 2020, https://apnews.com/article/georgia-lawsuits-elec-tions-election-2020-atlanta-e44bf5301bce5d0001dd696f82c373e0.

46   "New GA. Project v. Raffensperger," https://www.casemine.com/judgement/us/5f7aeee14653d05df39f3459.

47   Rudyard Kipling, "If," public domain.

48   Chris Joyner, "Trump's Pick for U.S. Attorney in Georgia Dismisses Election Fraud Claims: 'There's Just Nothing to Them.'" *The Atlanta Journal-Constitution*, January 12, 2021, https://www.ajc.com/news/trumps-pick-for-us-attorney-in-georgia-dismisses-election-fraud-claims-theres-just-nothing-to-them/7JMIL-37WANHWXCZD4FTJXH4CIQ/.

49   Ibid.

50   Amy Gardner and Matt Zapotosky, "U.S. Attorney in Georgia: 'There's Just Nothing To' Claims of Election Fraud," *The Washington Post*, January 12, 2021, https://www.washingtonpost.com/politics/us-attorney-georgia-fraud/2021/01/12/45a527c6-5526-11eb-a817-e5e7f8a406d6_story.html.

51   Harper Neidig, "Georgia Judge Throws Out Trump Campaign Lawsuit on Absentee Ballots," *The Hill*, November 5, 2020, https://thehill.com/regulation/court-battles/524634-georgia-judge-throws-out-trump-campaign-lawsuit-on-absentee-ballots.

52   "Election Security Rumor Vs. Reality," Cybersecurity & Infrastructure Security Agency, https://www.cisa.gov/rumorcontrol.

53   Ibid.

54   "Statement from CISA Director Krebs Following Final Day of Voting," Cyber-security & Infrastructure Security Agency, Last revised: January 21, 2021, https://www.cisa.gov/news/2020/11/04/statement-cisa-director-krebs-following-fi-nal-day-voting.

55   "Georgia Press Conference on Election Count Updates Transcript November 6," Rev.com, November 6, 2020, https://www.rev.com/blog/transcripts/geor-gia-press-conference-on-election-count-updates-transcript-november-6.

56   Ibid.

57   Ibid.

58   Ibid.

59   Thomas Barrabi, "Trump Campaign Taps Rep. Doug Collins to Lead Recount Team in Georgia," FoxNews, November 8, 2020, https://www.foxnews.com/politics/trump-campaign-doug-collins-georgia-recount

60   "Ga. Secretary of State Responds to Calls for His Resignation," WTOC, November 9, 2020, https://www.wtoc.com/2020/11/09/senators-calling-resignation-ga-secretary-state/.

61   Donald J. Trump (@realDonaldTrump), Twitter, November 9, 2020, See archive at: https://www.thetrumparchive.com/?results=1&searchbox=%22"Georgia+will+be+a+big+presidential+win%2C+as+it+was+the+night+of+the+%22.

62   "Ga. Secretary of State Responds to Calls for His Resignation," WTOC, November 9, 2020, https://www.wtoc.com/2020/11/09/senators-calling-resignation-ga-secretary-state/.

63   Angelina Velasquez, "Georgia GOP Chairman, Sen. Doug Collins Demand Recount of Ballots," CBS46, November 10, 2020, https://www.cbs46.com/news/georgia-gop-chairman-sen-doug-collins-demand-recount-of-ballots/article_36905272-2391-11eb-88e8-03bae36abdbf.html.

64   Jonathan Raymond, "Georgia Sec. State's Office Says It's 'Not Seeing Any Widespread Irregularities,'" 11Alive, November 6, 2020, https://www.11alive.com/article/news/politics/elections/georgia-vote-counting-integrity-secretary-of-state-office/85-af643ae6-77a2-4f9d-8801-684913bb5af0.

65   "Georgia Secretary of State Brad Raffensperger Press Conference Transcript: Announces Hand Recount," Rev.com, November 11, 2020, https://www.rev.com/blog/transcripts/georgia-secretary-of-state-brad-raffensperger-press-conference-transcript-announces-hand-recount.

66   Ibid.

67   Ibid.

68   Ibid.

69   Jim Galloway, "Opinion: The Georgia Secretary of State Who Insists that Two Plus Two Still Equals Four," The Atlanta Journal-Constitution, November 10, 2020, https://www.ajc.com/politics/politics-blog/opinion-the-georgia-secretary-of-state-who-insists-that-two-plus-two-still-equals-four/OI6TGTORTJGNVLFSIYZQWK52YA/.

70   Ibid.

71   Donald J. Trump (@realDonaldTrump), Twitter, November 12, 2020, See archive at: https://www.thetrumparchive.com/?results=1&searchbox=%22Must+see+%40seanhannity+takedown+of+the+horrible%2C+inaccurate+and+anything+but+secure+Dominion+Voting+System%22.

72   Donald J. Trump (@realDonaldTrump), Twitter, November 12, 2020, See archive at: https://www.thetrumparchive.com/?results=1&searchbox=%22"REPORT%3A+DOMINION+DELETED+2.7+MILLION+TRUMP+VOTES+NATIONWIDE.+DATA+ANALYSIS+FIND-

S+221%2C000+PENNSYLVANIA+VOTES+SWITCHED+FROM+PRESI-DENT+TRUMP+TO+BIDEN%22.

73   "Joint Statement from Elections Infrastructure Government Coordinating Council & The Election Infrastructure Sector Coordinating Executive Committees," CISA, November 12, 2020, https://www.cisa.gov/news/2020/11/12/joint-statement-elections-infrastructure-government-coordinating-council-election.

74   Ibid.

75   Kate Brumback, "Sidney Powell Unrelenting in Legal Battle on Trump's Behalf," AP, December 10, 2020, https://apnews.com/article/election-2020-joe-biden-donald-trump-georgia-lawsuits-0ed38af7f94b596308475aa8b28c871c.

76   Donald J. Trump (@realDonaldTrump), Twitter, November 13, 2020, See archive at: https://www.thetrumparchive.com/?results=1&searchbox=%22Georgia+Secretary+of+State%2C+a+so-called+Republican+%28RINO%29%2C+won't+let+the+people+checking+the+ballots+see+the+signatures+for+fraud.+Why%3F+Without+this+the+whole+process+is+very+unfair+%22

77   "A Declaration of Conscience," United States Senate, June 1, 1950, https://www.senate.gov/about/powers-procedures/investigations/mccarthy-hearings/a-declaration-of-conscience.htm.

78   "NASS Margaret Chase Smith American Democracy Award," NASS, https://www.nass.org/node/179.

79   Chris Krebs (@CISAKrebs), Twitter, November 17, 2020, https://twitter.com/cisakrebs/status/1328741106624901120?lang=en.

80   Donald J. Trump (@realDonaldTrump), Twitter, November 17, 2020, See archive at: https://www.thetrumparchive.com/?results=1&dates=%5B%222020-11-17%22%2C%222020-11-18%22%5D.

81   Jeff Amy, "Georgia Elections Chief Battles Fellow Republicans, Trump," AP, November 17, 2020, https://apnews.com/article/raffensperger-battles-fellow-gop-trump-a36b023d910814fa8c20d5e62d8ad645.

82   "The Georgia Risk-Limiting Audit/Hand Tally: A Carter Center Observation Report," The Carter Center, November 2020, https://www.cartercenter.org/resources/pdfs/news/peace_publications/democracy/georgia-audit-final-report-033121.pdf.

83   Calvin Woodward and Ali Swenson, "AP Fact Check: Trump's Flailing Effort Resting on Mendacity," AP, November 21, 2020, https://apnews.com/article/election-2020-ap-fact-check-joe-biden-donald-trump-technology-16e2f349873efcef-5c69e749b677d85c.

84   "Rudy Giuliani Trump Campaign Press Conference Transcript November 19: Election Fraud Claims," Rev.com, November 19, 2020, https://www.rev.com/blog/transcripts/rudy-giuliani-trump-campaign-press-conference-transcript-november-19-election-fraud-claims.

85   GA Secretary of State Brad Raffensperger, "Lin Wood Lawsuit," Facebook, November 15, 2020, https://m.facebook.com/GASecretaryofState/photos/a.2134798756635689/3559519377496946/?type=3&p=60.

86   Glenn Kessler, "Fact-checking the Craziest News Conference of the Trump Pres-

idency," *The Washington Post*," November 19, 2020, https://www.washingtonpost.com/politics/2020/11/19/fact-checking-craziest-news-conference-trump-presidency/.

87   Jan Wolfe, "U.S. Judiciary, Shaped by Trump, Thwarts His Election Challenges," *Reuters*, December 1, 2020, https://www.reuters.com/article/us-usa-election-trump-judges/u-s-judiciary-shaped-by-trump-thwarts-his-election-challenges-idUSKBN28B60O.

88   "Georgia Recount Announcement Transcript November 20: Biden Wins," Rev.com, November 20, 2020, https://www.rev.com/blog/transcripts/georgia-recount-announcement-transcript-november-20-biden-wins.

89   Jonathan Raymond, "Lawsuit Filed Week after Election to Stop Certification Dismissed by 11th Circuit Court of Appeals," 11 Alive, December 5, 2020, https://www.11alive.com/article/news/politics/elections/lin-wood-suit-dismissed-by-11th-circuit/85-4cc305df-c5c8-43ef-9e4b-cdf71bf24475.

90   "Wood v. Raffensperger," Casetext, https://casetext.com/case/wood-v-raffensperger.

91   Ibid.

92   Ibid.

93   Josh Feldman, "Trump Lawyer Sidney Powell Accuses Georgia Gov. Brian Kemp and Bernie Sanders of Complicity in Bonkers Voting Machine Conspiracy," Media ITE, November 22, 2020, https://www.mediaite.com/election-2020/trump-lawyer-sidney-powell-accuses-georgia-gov-brian-kemp-and-bernie-sanders-of-complicity-in-bonkers-voting-machine-conspiracy/.

94   Eric Tucker, "Trump Campaign Legal Team Distances Itself from Powell," AP News, November 22, 2020, https://apnews.com/article/trump-campaign-distances-sidney-powell-c74165d465cf28b5478a65bd267fde29.

95   "Powell Lawsuit in Michigan Alleges 'Dominion Computer Fraud' and 'Illegal Conduct' by Election Workers," Easy Reader, https://easyreader.org/article/page/theepochtimes/sidney-powell-files-suit-in-michigan-alleging-dominion-computer-fraud-and-illegal-conduct-by-election-workers_3594298.html.

96   Administration of Donald J. Trump, 2020, "Remarks During a Video Teleconference with United States Servicemembers and Exchange with Reporters," Authenticated U.S. Government Information, November 26, 2020, https://www.govinfo.gov/content/pkg/DCPD-202000864/pdf/DCPD-202000864.pdf

97   "Fired Director of U.S. Cyber Agency Chris Krebs Explains Why He Says Vote Was 'Most Secure . . .'" *60 Minutes*, November 29, 2020, https://www.youtube.com/watch?v=YzBJJ1sxtEA.

98   "Georgia Election Official Gabriel Sterling: 'Someone's Going to Get Killed' Transcript," Rev.com, December 1, 2020, https://www.rev.com/blog/transcripts/georgia-election-official-gabriel-sterling-someones-going-to-get-killed-transcript.

99   Andrew Mark Miller, "Flynn Shares Petition Urging Trump to Suspend the Constitution and Hold an Election Re-Vote Overseen by Military," *Washington Examiner*, December 3, 2020, https://www.washingtonexaminer.com/news/flynn-shares-petition-urging-trump-to-suspend-the-constitution-and-hold-an-election-re-vote-overseen-by-military.

100   Michael Balsamo, "Disputing Trump, Barr Says No Widespread Election Fraud," AP, December 1, 2020, https://apnews.com/article/barr-no-widespread-election-fraud-b1f1488796c9a98c4b1a9061a6c7f49d.

101   Donald J. Trump (@realDonaldTrump), Twitter, December 1, 2020, See archive at: https://www.thetrumparchive.com/?results=1&searchbox=%22Rigged+Election.+-Show+signatures+and+envelopes.+Expose+the+massive+voter+fraud+in+Georgia.+What+is+Secretary+of+State+and+%40BrianKempGA+afraid+of.+They+know+what+we'll+find%21%21%21%22.

102   "Georgia Senate Election Hearing Transcript December 3," Rev.com, December 3, 2020, https://www.rev.com/blog/transcripts/georgia-senate-election-hearing-transcript-december-3.

103   Ibid.

104   Scot Pelley, "Georgia Secretary of State Describes Call Where Trump Pressured Him to Find Evidence of Voter Fraud," *60 Minutes*, January 10, 2021, https://www.cbsnews.com/news/georgia-election-brad-raffensperger-60-minutes-2021-01-10/.

105   Jonathan Raymond, "Georgia Election Official Says Trump Is 'Flat Out, 100 Percent, Four Square Wrong' About Consent Decree," ABC10, November 17, 2020, https://www.abc10.com/article/news/politics/elections/georgia-consent-decree-election-official-says-trump-wrong/85-db462666-11d4-46c1-97e4-18d9b-f79e365.

106   Donald J. Trump (@realDonaldTrump), Twitter, November 14, 2020, See archive at: https://www.thetrumparchive.com/?results=1&searchbox=%22The+Consent+Decree+signed+by+the+Georgia+Secretary+of+State%2C+with+the+approval+of+Governor+%40BrianKempGA%2C+at+the+urging+of+%40stacey-abrams%2C+makes+it+impossible+to+check+%26+match+signatures+on+ballots+and+envelopes%2C+etc.+They+knew+they+were+going+to+cheat.+Must+expose+real+signatures%21%22.

107   "House Bill 316 (As Passed House and Senate)," https://www.legis.ga.gov/api/legislation/document/20192020/184671.

108   "Absentee Voting: A Guide for Registered Voters," Georgia Secretary of State Elections Division, 2020, https://sos.ga.gov/admin/files/Absentee_Voting_A_Guide_for_Registered_Voters_2020.pdf.

109   "Donald J. Trump v. Brad Raffensperger," https://studylib.net/doc/25438983/verified-petition-to-contest-georgia-election.

110   Justin Gray (@JustinGrayWSB), Twitter, December 4, 2020, https://twitter.com/justingraywsb/status/1334919773352812547?lang=en.

111   Ibid.

112   USCA11 Case: 20-14418, Date filed: December 5, 2020, https://media.ca11.uscourts.gov/opinions/pub/files/202014418.pdf.

113   Camille Caldera, "Fact Check: A 37-vote Change in Georgia Was the Result of Human Error, Not Vote-flipping," *USA Today*, December 8, 2020, https://www.usatoday.com/story/news/factcheck/2020/12/08/fact-check-vote-change-human-error-not-vote-flipping/6495143002/.

114   "Secretary of State's Office Debunks Ware County Voting Machine Story," *Albany*

Herald, December 8, 2020, https://www.albanyherald.com/features/secretary-of-state-s-office-debunks-ware-county-voting-machine-story/article_babb913e-397f-11eb-b6d7-47edca2fdf5a.html.

115   Ali Swenson, "Dominion Machines Didn't 'Flip' Votes in Ware County, Georgia," AP, December 7, 2020, https://apnews.com/article/fact-checking-9773239691.

116   "Secretary of State's Office Debunks Ware County Voting Machine Story," Georgia Secretary of State Office, https://sos.ga.gov/index.php/elections/secretary_of_states_office_debunks_ware_county_voting_machine_story

117   "Georgia Election Officials Briefing Transcript December 7: Will Recertify Election Results Today," Rev.com, December 7, 2020, https://www.rev.com/blog/transcripts/georgia-election-officials-briefing-transcript-december-7-will-recertify-election-results-today.

118   Ibid.

119   Ibid.

120   Mark Niesse and David Wickert, "Judge Dismisses Lawsuit Challenging Biden's Win in Georgia," *The Atlanta Journal-Constitution*, December 7, 2020, https://www.ajc.com/politics/breaking-judge-dismisses-lawsuit-challenging-bidens-win-in-georgia/UXSI5WUROJA4JHLTVTJ6UWNWOM/.

121   "Campaign 2020: Georgia Final 2020 Presidential Recount Results," C-SPAN, December 7, 2020, https://www.c-span.org/video/?507078-1/georgia-final-2020-presidential-recount-results.

122   "Texas Attorney General Ken Paxton Sues Battleground States in Supreme Court, Says Changes to 2020 Election Laws 'Unconstitutional,'" CBS DFW, December 8, 2020, https://dfw.cbslocal.com/2020/12/08/texas-attorney-general-ken-paxton-sues-battleground-states-says-changes-to-2020-election-laws-unconstitutional/.

123   Ibid.

124   Jessica Szilagyi, "Georgia Senators Applaud State of Texas Election Challenge," AllOnGeorgia, December 8, 2020, https://allongeorgia.com/georgia-state-politics/georgia-senators-applaud-state-of-texas-election-challenge/.

125   "State of Texas v. Commonwealth of Pennsylvania, State of Georgia, State of Michigan, and State of Wisconsin," SupremeCourt.gov, https://www.supremecourt.gov/DocketPDF/22/22O155/163383/20201210145849997_Georgia%20--%20Brief%20in%20Opposition.pdf.

126   Donald J. Trump (@realDonaldTrump), Twitter, December 9, 2020, See archive at: https://www.thetrumparchive.com/?results=1&searchbox=%22We+will+be+INTERVENING+in+the+Texas+%28plus+many+other+states%29+case.+This+is+the+big+one.+Our+Country+needs+a+victory%21%22.

127   Michelle Ye Hee Lee, "Here's What Happened When a Georgia Lawmaker Scrutinized the Trump Campaign's List of Allegedly Illegal Votes," *The Seattle Times*, March 10, 2021, https://www.seattletimes.com/nation-world/nation-politics/heres-what-happened-when-a-georgia-lawmaker-scrutinized-the-trump-campaigns-list-of-allegedly-illegal-votes/.

128   "Texas v. Pennsylvania," SupremeCourt.gov, https://www.supremecourt.gov/search.

aspx?filename=/docket/docketfiles/html/public/22o155.html.

129 Zack Budryk, "Georgia House Speaker Calls for Secretary of State to Be Chosen by General Assembly, Not Voters," *The Hill*, December 10, 2020, https://thehill. com/homenews/state-watch/529770-georgia-house-speaker-calls-for-secretary-of-state-to-be-chosen-by.

130 Jessica Szilagyi, "As Georgia SOL Launches Signature Match Audit, Other Republicans Keep Raffensperger at a Distance," AllonGeorgia, December 15, 2020, https://allongeorgia.com/georgia-state-politics/as-georgia-sos-launches-signature-match-audit-other-republicans-keep-raffensperger-at-a-distance/.

131 "The Georgia Secretary of State's Office holds . . ."WRCB Channel 3, December 14, 2020, https://www.facebook.com/106111954344/videos/822746965187964.

132 Donald J. Trump (@realDonaldTrump), Twitter, December 23, 2020, See archive at: https://www.thetrumparchive.com/?results=1&search-box=%22They+are+slow+walking+the+signature+verification+in+Geor-gia.+They+don't+want+results+to+get+out+prior+to+January+6th.+They+-know+what+they+are+trying+so+hard+to+hide.+Terrible+people%21+%22.

133 "Georgia Secretary of State Recording of Trump Phone Call to Election Investi-gator," American Oversight, March 10, 2021, https://www.americanoversight.org/document/georgia-secretary-of-state-recording-of-trump-phone-call-to-election-investigator.

134 Ibid.

135 Ibid.

136 "3rd Strike Against Voter Fraud Claims Means They're Out After Signature Audit Finds No Fraud," Georgia Secretary of State, https://sos.ga.gov/index.php/elections/3rd_strike_against_voter_fraud_claims_means_theyre_out_after_signa-ture_audit_finds_no_fraud.

137 Ibid.

138 Ibid.

139 Ibid.

140 Donald J. Trump (@realDonaldTrump), Twitter, December 29, 2020, See archive at: https://www.thetrumparchive.com/?results=1&searchbox-=%22I+love+the+great+state+of+Georgia%2C+but+the+people+who+run+it%2C+-from+the+Governor%2C+%40BrianKempGA%2C+to+the+Secre-tary+of+State%2C+are+a+complete+disaster+and+don't+have+a+clu-e%2C+or+worse.+%22.

141 Donald J. Trump (@realDonaldTrump), Twitter, December 29, 2020, See archive at: https://www.thetrumparchive.com/?results=1&searchbox=%22Now+it+turns+out+that+Brad+R's+brother+works+for+China+and+they+definite-ly+don't+want+"Trump".+So+disgusting%21%22.

142 "Where They Are Now," Fast Company, March 1, 2004, https://www.fastcompany.com/48220/where-they-are-now.

143 Christopher Boyle, "Inventor Jovan Pulitzer Claims He Was Bribed '$10 Million Dollars' Not to Investigate Allegations of Voter Fraud in 2020 Elections," *The Pub-*

lished Reporter, April 12, 2021, https://www.publishedreporter.com/2021/04/12/inventor-jovan-pulitzer-claims-he-was-bribed-10-million-dollars-not-to-investigate-allegations-of-voter-fraud/.

144   "Georgia Sec. of State's Office Warns Election Hearings Are Depressing Turnout," 13WMAZ, January 1, 2021, https://www.13wmaz.com/article/news/politics/georgia-sec-of-states-office-warns-election-hearings-are-depressing-turnout/93-c09a837b-62e5-430f-92ef-f27a8beb5d77.

145   "State Senators Hear Testimony of Failed Treasure Hunter," *Albany Herald*, January 2, 2021, https://www.albanyherald.com/news/state-senators-hear-testimony-of-failed-treasure-hunter/article_4f4d983a-4d06-11eb-aa34-fbf12beb75c3.html.

146   Kyle Cheney and Josh Gerstein, "Georgia Fights Latest Trump Suit to Overturn November Election," Politico, January 4, 2021, https://www.politico.com/news/2021/01/04/trump-georgia-overturn-kemp-454925.

147   Amy Gardner and Paulina Firozi, "Here's the Full Transcript and Audio of the Call Between Trump and Raffensperger," *The Washington Post*, January 5, 2021, https://www.washingtonpost.com/politics/trump-raffensperger-call-transcript-georgia-vote/2021/01/03/2768e0cc-4ddd-11eb-83e3-322644d82356_story.html.

148   Donald J. Trump (@realDonaldTrump), Twitter, January 3, 2021, See archive at: https://www.thetrumparchive.com/?results=1&searchbox=%22I+spoke+to+Secretary+of+State+Brad+Raffensperger+yesterday+about+Fulton+County+and+voter+fraud+in+Georgia.+He+was+unwilling%2C+or+unable%2C+to+answer+questions+such+as+the+"ballots+under+table"+scam%2C+ballot+destruction%2C+out+of+state+"voters"%2C+dead+voters%2C+and+more.+He+has+no+clue%21%22.

149   GA Secretary of State Brad Raffensperger (@GaSecofState), Twitter, January 3, 2021, https://twitter.com/gasecofstate/status/1345753643593687040?lang=en.

150   Amy Gardner and Paulina Firozi, "Here's the Full Transcript and Audio of the Call Between Trump and Raffensperger," *The Washington Post*, January 5, 2021, https://www.washingtonpost.com/politics/trump-raffensperger-call-transcript-georgia-vote/2021/01/03/2768e0cc-4ddd-11eb-83e3-322644d82356_story.html.

151   "Message from the Senate; Congressional Record Vol. 167, No. 4, House of Representatives, January 6, 2021, Congress.gov, https://www.congress.gov/congressional-record/2021/1/6/house-section/article/H94-1.

152   "Trump's Phone Call with Georgia's Top Election Official," *60 Minutes*, January 12, 2021, https://www.youtube.com/watch?v=s1u8F6ERqqE.

153   Ibid.

154   Ibid.